KAFFE FASSETT'S
MUSEUM QUILTS

KAFFE FASSETT'S MUSEUM QUILTS

DESIGNS INSPIRED BY THE
VICTORIA & ALBERT MUSEUM

WITH LIZA PRIOR LUCY

The Taunton Press

I would like to dedicate this book to
Liza Prior Lucy who gave me the original
idea for it

RIGHT The *Jockey's Cap Baby Quilt* (see page 57).
FAR RIGHT Kaffe Fassett on location.
PAGE I The *Wedding Snowball Quilt* (see page 32).
PAGE 2 The *Mariner's Compass Quilt* in front of a Chinese screen in the
Victoria and Albert Museum in London (see page 63).

The Taunton Press
Inspiration for hands-on living®

The Taunton Press
63 South Main St., PO Box 5506
Newtown, CT 06470-5506
www.taunton.com

First published in the United Kingdom in 2005 by Ebury Press, Random House
20 Vauxhall Bridge Road, London SW1V 2SA

Editor: Sally Harding
Art Director: Christine Wood
Flat-Shot photography: Jon Stewart
Special still-life photography: Debbie Patterson
Copy editor: Ali Glenny
Diagram and template illustrations: Anthony Duke
Techniques illustrations: Kate Simunek

ISBN: 1-56158-754-0

Printed and bound in China by C&C Offset Printing Co.,Ltd.

CONTENTS

INTRODUCTION

As long as I can remember I have been amazed and delighted by museums that give space to the decorative arts. Fine art is an ongoing passion and has a permanent space in my life, but decoration on everyday objects has become more and more important to me as I mature. Imagine my excitement when I first stumbled on the vast treasure trove in London that is the Victoria and Albert Museum, totally dedicated to celebrating decorative arts from around the world. It has been a great mansion of inspiration for me ever since I settled in London in 1964. I wandered its enormous galleries on floor after floor and came into contact with the finest porcelain, furniture, musical instruments and ornate jewelry, and, best of all, textiles of every description and from every culture. The dedicated textile rooms, especially the patchwork quilts housed there, had a particular fascination for me.

Those early V&A wanderings gave inspiration to my work. I started out as a painter of still-lifes featuring pattern on pattern – often with old patchworks as a base to the arrangements of patterned crockery. From these paintings I went on to design intricate, colourful textiles and publish books on needlepoint, knitting, interiors and patchwork. In 1988 the V&A held a large exhibition of my work, augmented with inspirational pottery and glass from the museum's collection.

In the early 1990s Liza Lucy, the co-author on my two previous patchwork books, opened a door when she suggested we search the V&A collection of English quilts to do a book of contemporary adaptations. I had seen the *Clamshell Quilt* (see page 46) and was totally fascinated by it, so eagerly anticipated the treasures lurking in the archive. We made a date to view them and were certainly not disappointed. When I saw what the V&A had behind the scenes, I was thrilled at the prospect of using these patchworks as a jumping off point. As one personal extravaganza after another was carefully unfolded, we knew without a doubt that the material for the next book lay on that viewing table. The ingenuity of old quilt makers in creating exquisitely fascinating arrangements of fabric in geometric or figurative motifs is always stimulating. The period from the mid 1700s up to 1900 was particularly creative. If I were a museum curator, I could easily make this period of quilt making my life's work.

At first the plan was to do a very personal interpretation of each quilt, but the more I studied the originals and translated them into contemporary fabrics, the more I perceived how satisfying the exact original patch layouts were. When the colour moods were changed, the physical formats seemed to grow into quite different entities. Sarah Wyatt's simple, utilitarian quilt (see page 20), for example, becomes as showy as a Moulin Rouge dancing girl when done in scarlet, black and over-blown rose prints. So whenever possible I have tried to stick closely to the original geometric format, simplifying only a few intricate patches to make them more accessible to modern patchworkers.

In all my work, I like to show my readers and makers a few different versions of an idea to indicate that many more versions can be discovered if they will play with colour schemes. Featured in this book are not only my one or two versions of each chosen V&A quilt, but also the originals in the elegant palettes that attracted me in the first place. Sometimes I have stuck closely to the old palette, such as on the *Jockey's Cap Baby Quilt* (see page 57) and the *Mariner's Compass Quilt* (see page 63), but I couldn't resist seeing how much a set format changes with fresh colour thinking.

Liza's studio in Pennsylvania was the site of most of the design work on this new collection. I would arrive for a week or two's stay and in less than an hour we would have the entire house strewn with fabrics and paper

ABOVE My *Lone Star Quilt* in the Victoria and Albert Museum's Sculpture Court. The large Italian painting reflects so many of the colours in the quilt. (See pages 36 and 37 for more about this quilt.)

patterns. Our two massive work walls — screens made of insulating board covered in camel-toned flannel — would be quickly covered. As Liza cut pieces, I would arrange and rearrange them until the colours sang to both our satisfaction. We would break off from time to time to go fabric hunting in local shops or to visit friends with collections of old quilts, which we would drool over as we picked up fresh ideas. There is always so much to learn from the old colour combinations.

What will be really exciting to me is to see you take the traditional quilt formats in the following pages and imbue them with your own choice of fabrics. Since the publication of my first book on patchwork, *Glorious Patchwork*, I have travelled the world giving workshops on my quilt designs and been delighted by the sheer variety of personal versions that participants have come up with. I look forward to your interpretations of this new collection.

UTILITY QUILTS

Although I am known for extravagant production numbers in the various disciplines I tackle, such as knitting, needlepoint and mosaics, I have a real enthusiasm for designing simple everyday objects. To make a practical utensil joyful to the eye is to make life a deal less humdrum. I have often found myself deeply grateful for a bit of fretwork, a flower painted on a cupboard door or a patterned edging on a pillow in an otherwise plain hotel room. The very simplest patchwork quilt can give an intensely personal touch to any room, particularly a neutral one.

For the seven quilts in this chapter, I chose for my jumping off point the extra-simple patchwork formats that tantalized me at the V&A. Although they are all quick to stitch, like my Sarah's Gypsy Throw (left and above), they are still brilliantly eye-catching and exciting despite their paired-down simplicity.

These Utility Quilts look like functional everyday objects – and they could, indeed, be used as a car or picnic blanket, a couch throw or a table covering – but they are anything but staid. Their energy makes them a delight at every new viewing.

Make one and see!

LEFT AND ABOVE The aged pink walls and the old masters in their gold frames provide a rich setting, indeed, for one of my versions of the V&A's Sarah Wyatt quilt, *Sarah's Gypsy Throw* (see pages 18–23).

MY INSPIRATION

ABOVE The source idea for my *Columns Quilts* is actually this elegant backing on a nineteenth-century crazy patchwork quilt that I spotted in the V&A collection. I fell in love with the beautiful melting tones of the antique large-scale prints. The silver-grey and beige motifs and old fresco hues of terracotta, sage and gold with depths of charcoal and dark lacquer red made me green with jealousy. If only I could achieve such a rapturous harmony!

RIGHT This detail of the V&A's quilt backing shows the striking quality of nineteenth-century fabric prints. The twists and turns of the large-scale leaves and flowers, in a chalky harmonious palette, make the wide fabric strips merge in a most mysterious way. To think this was meant to be glimpsed only when the crazy patchwork front of the quilt was inadvertently folded over.

DARK FLORAL COLUMNS

ABOVE My *Floral Column Quilts* are the easiest to make of all the patchworks in the book (see page 74 for the instructions). Start collecting the boldest large-scale prints you can, in sympathetic colours, if you want to run up this *Dark Floral Columns Quilt*.

The large-scale flower prints used for the second, fifth and ninth strips from the left are three different colourways of a fabric I designed for my patchwork fabric collection called *August Rose* (see page 159 for fabric suppliers). It sits snugly between two nineteenth-century reproduction fabrics. When you make your own version of this quilt, pin scraps of your prints side by side on the wall, then stand back to have a good look. Keep rearranging till you find combinations that make each of the prints really sing – a print on its own may seem to lack pizzazz, but sitting next to just the right companion it can suddenly show hidden depths.

LIGHT FLORAL COLUMNS

RIGHT AND BELOW The fabrics in the V&A inspiration for this quilt are knockout stunning and flow so effortlessly together (see page 10). After making a dark version of the quilt (see page 11), I made another attempt to recreate the flow of the original in lighter tones. My *Light Floral Columns Quilt* may not reach the heights of the antique quilt, but it would look charming in a densely wallpapered bedroom. (See page 74 for the instructions for this quilt.)

LEFT The *Dark Floral Columns*, which has a deeper, richer palette than the light version on the right. The purples, rusts and sages work well in this old room.

MY INSPIRATION

ABOVE AND RIGHT I've seen many wonderful antique quilts in Wales, but this is the only one in the V&A collection. The big plain border, in two shades of brown, allowed the quilter to really go to town creating a pressed leather look. Wonderfully dramatic, the black fabrics give such depth to the toasty, leather tones. The grey-blue print is just right for the composition, too, giving a cool toning to all those warm browns. All of the patches are cotton and most of these were glazed. Two large-scale prints in the quilt centre (see right) date from 1815 and 1820, and the most recent print is an 1840s rosebud pattern.

PAGES 14 AND 15 My *Welsh Quilt* hanging looks very much at home with this old classical architecture.

WELSH QUILT

ABOVE AND RIGHT I used all my own fabrics on this
contemporary version of the nineteenth-century quilt and
hope the colours are as harmonious as those of the original.
My *Lotus Leaf* print in old brown tones at the centre is quite
a lively touch. I tried to use the same balance of stripes
and floral prints as the original. My Indian woven *Ikat Wash*
fabric gives the outer border a rippling sense of movement.
Faithfully following the format of the early nineteenth-century
original, the border at the top of the quilt is deeper than the
bottom border so that it can be wrapped around the pillows
at the top of the bed. (See pages 75–77 for the instructions.)

SARAH'S PASTEL
QUILT

LEFT AND RIGHT *Sarah's Pastel Quilt*
was made slightly larger than the
original (see page 20) to suit the
size of today's beds. (See page 21
for more about this patchwork.)

MY INSPIRATION

ABOVE AND RIGHT Long borders of basic dot prints
frame the bold layout of pinwheels on this English
V&A quilt. The all-over vocabulary of dots and stripes
subtly enlivens the simple geometry. The colour is a
little restrained for my taste, but it proved a good
structure to play with. Since there are hearts in the
quilting, it is thought that the quilt was made to
celebrate an engagement, marriage or birth, or as a
gift for a young girl. The maker signed it in cross stitch
on the back 'Sarah Wyatt 1801'.

SARAH'S PASTEL QUILT

ABOVE AND LEFT For *Sarah's Pastel Quilt*, I started
from the almost monotone of the original and
imbued it with a soft colouring that I hope has a
little more life. A mosaic splashback that I made
for my sink, using mostly white china with accents
of pale pastels, was the starting point for this
colour mood. The toile prints fade gently into
other pastel prints to create a soft pastel
confection that looks charmingly old-fashioned.
(See pages 78 and 79 for the instructions.)

SARAH'S GYPSY THROW

ABOVE AND RIGHT After I made the soft, easy-on-the-eye version of this basic quilt (see *Sarah's Pastel Quilt* on the previous page), I thought I would do something really exotic and as totally different as one could get from the ticking-like stripe and dotty fabrics of the original. I had just designed the red dot *Double Ikat* fabric (in the outer border) and felt it set off the rose prints with spicy richness. (Turn to pages 78 and 79 for the instructions.)

MY INSPIRATION

ABOVE AND LEFT Attributed to the second half of the eighteenth century, this English V&A coverlet is made up of strips of silk ribbons – they look like hair ribbons to me. Many of the ribbons are patterned with a variety of checks and stripes. The horizontal stripes on some of the patches provide a crisp contrast to the long, thin brick shapes. The quilting is a joyous series of circles and fan shapes. When I saw this quilt for the first time, I was determined to try out the simple geometry of elongated bricks.

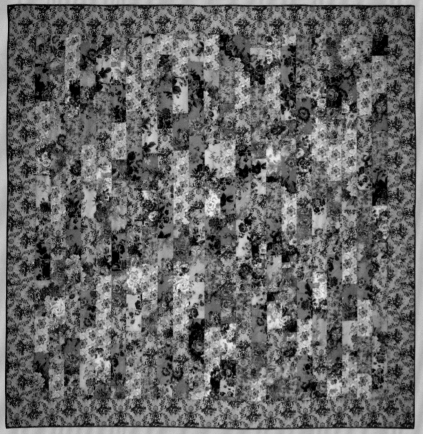

FLORAL BRICKS QUILT

ABOVE AND LEFT A collection of rosy fabrics spilling
into each other seemed perfect for the simple bricks
format. Unfortunately, to my eye now, the border lets
it down a bit, as it is a fabric used in the quilt as well.
If I did it again I would choose a totally different print
to frame it all, perhaps a very large-scale floral print,
as a foil to the prints in the bricks. Keep this in mind
when choosing fabrics for your own version. (See
pages 80 and 81 for the instructions.)

BABY BRICKS QUILT

ABOVE AND RIGHT This most basic of quilts uses mostly ticking-like stripes; all the fabrics come from my patchwork fabric collection (see page 159 for suppliers). The layout would look even finer and more intense if made with a wide selection of shirt fabrics. Another version worth trying would be a combination of my *Floral Stripes* fabric along with my *Paisley Stripes*, all framed in a bolder *Roman Stripe*. (See pages 80 and 81 for the instructions.)

TRADITIONAL QUILTS

When I got involved in designing patchwork quilts, I very quickly found it wasn't the expressionistic contemporary ones that got my attention. Neither were the simple two- and three-colour contrast quilts of interest to me. Every time I'd find myself stopped in my tracks by a quilt, it would always be because of a very simple traditional layout made up of lots of scrap fabrics in mesmerizing colours. Simple squares, rectangles, diamonds and triangles constantly delight me with the unexpected variations that make them appear so fresh and intriguing.

In this chapter I hope you enjoy the different approaches to basic snowball, star and hourglass blocks, plus the very easy-to-make squares-on-point (see pages 41, 42 and 48). Because these traditional quilts have pretty straightforward instructions you can really go to town on the colouring and mood of your prints. They can be lavish (usually my preference) or beautifully restrained and minimal if that is required.

This book gave me the chance to design a special new range of fabrics. I looked at lots of the old prints in the V&A quilts and came up with some that have the same mood. The *Lone Star, Clamshell* and the *Square Clamshell Quilts* feature the best of this collection (see pages 37, 47 and 49).

LEFT AND ABOVE The *Persian-Blue Stars Quilt* draped over the drawing room piano in a historic London house.

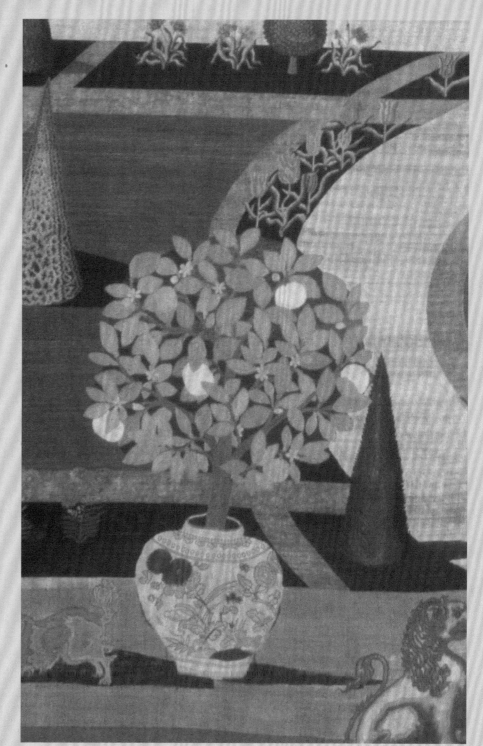

LEAFY SNOWBALL QUILT

LEFT Leafy porcelain, wallpaper and textiles always draw my eye. A quilt tablecloth done in leafy calico prints, featured in a book on Australian quilts, really stuck in my head. With this in mind, I decided to collect together every leafy print I had designed over the years and patch them all together. The *Leafy Snowball Quilt* is the result. One of the main inspirations for the rich fabric concoction in this quilt is the wonderful tapestries dotted around the V&A that feature gardens and woodland scenes. Saturated with a green colour scheme of fruits and foliage, the William Morris Room in the museum is also a good example of the mood I was after here. (See pages 82 and 83 for the instructions.)

MY INSPIRATION

ABOVE The detail here, from a V&A hanging, illustrates the lush leafiness that I find so appealing. Made for the Foley family of Stoke Edith, Herefordshire, England, the hanging is a linen canvas embroidered with silk and wool, and dated 1710–20. The format for the blocks in the *Leafy Snowball Quilt* came from the Averil Colby cushions on page 32.

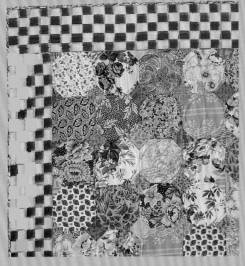

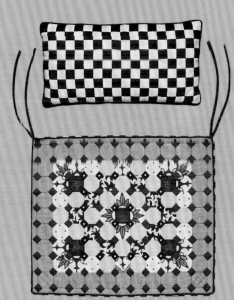

MY INSPIRATION

LEFT This rather prim, monochromatic use of the snowball block (below left) is a chair seat made by the English textile historian Averil Colby in 1953. It plays with mirror imaging in a precise way and gave us the excuse (since it is part of the V&A collection) to do our two adaptations of this wonderfully simple pattern, the *Leafy Snowball* and *Wedding Snowball Quilts*. The chair seat is a good example of 'fussy' cutting of the patterned fabrics, which can be very effective in mirror-image patchwork. The quilt borders are modelled on the simple chequerboard side and chair-back pads (above chair seat, left).

WEDDING SNOWBALL QUILT

ABOVE AND RIGHT Blue and white, as many fans will know, is a reoccurring theme in my design life. I've done versions in needlepoint, knitting, painting and patchwork. Here I took every blue-and-white fabric I could lay my hands on, raided Liza's considerable stash and combined them to create this frothy quilt. The small accent squares in chalky pastels give great warmth to the cool blue palette. The blue-and-white tiles with added tints in the V&A's Poynter Room (right) echoes the quilt perfectly. If you wish, use a printed chintz bouquet for the quilt centre instead of appliqué or omit the centre square all together and fill in with more snowball blocks. (See pages 84 and 85 for the instructions.)

MY INSPIRATION

ABOVE AND RIGHT This V&A quilt is almost Amish in its use of solid-coloured fabrics. It is thought to have been made by a fashionable dressmaker in the last quarter of the nineteenth century, as it is composed entirely of dress silks. These colours were fashionable in Britain at that time. I was captivated by the layout, with its framed and solid-coloured stars, and pinwheel-like two-colour versions. The large blue pointed border echoes the star shapes. I would love to see a version of this in reds, magentas and brilliant greens.

PERSIAN-BLUE STARS QUILT

ABOVE, RIGHT AND LEFT The V&A has an impressive collection of Persian-blue china. The cobalt blue, deep shades of turquoise and emerald green of this ancient pottery cry out to be used together. The original quilt didn't move me colourwise, but when that Persian-blue richness was fed into this design it really took on a dark glow. Being me, I couldn't resist adding a few patterned fabrics to the mix. (See pages 87–90 for the instructions.)

MY INSPIRATION

RIGHT This late-nineteenth-century bed cover is one of four American quilts in the V&A collection. I'm afraid I passed over it at first, because it is so limited in its fabrics. The contrast of navy blue with pink and yellow is quite crude, but the bold scale is irresistible as a layout. It is fascinating that practically the whole quilt is made up of one diamond patch shape. The quilting is a simple linear design that follows the diamonds. You will see from the *Lone Star Quilt* on the opposite page and the *Ode to Dale Evans* on page 39 how many adventures can be had with this basic traditional design.

BELOW A detail from my *Lone Star Quilt*, showing up close some of my own print designs.

LONE STAR QUILT

ABOVE Old single-star quilts are dazzling, especially when the prints bleed creatively into each other as they often do with this format. I tried to achieve that in my own version, the *Lone Star Quilt*. It is made up of my own prints, including the *Organic* and *Swiggle Stripes* designed specially for this book. Since each of these prints has four bands of different small prints on it, you get a lot of variety out of each colourway. The background is my *Roman Glass* print, which was inspired by some Roman glass fragments in the V&A glass galleries. (See pages 91–93 for the instructions.)

ODE TO DALE EVANS

ABOVE, LEFT AND FAR LEFT Every once in a while, a student shows up in
Liza's and my classes who is so talented that it knocks our socks off.
Claudia Chaback is a case in point. She has designed many original quilts
of her own, but I include her outrageous version of a lone star quilt
here because it is so refreshingly different from both mine and the V&A
original (see pages 36 and 37). The star is very unaffected and African in
mood, with its earthy contrast tones. The large-scale rose print is a truly
inspired background, reminiscent of a cowgirl outfit. I hope Claudia's
lone star inspires you to do your own personal version.

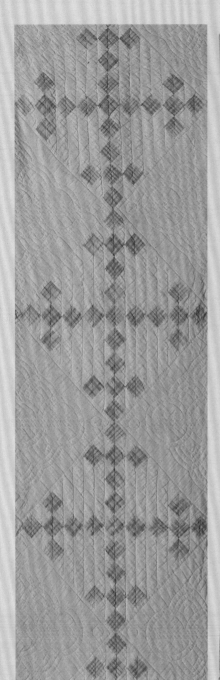

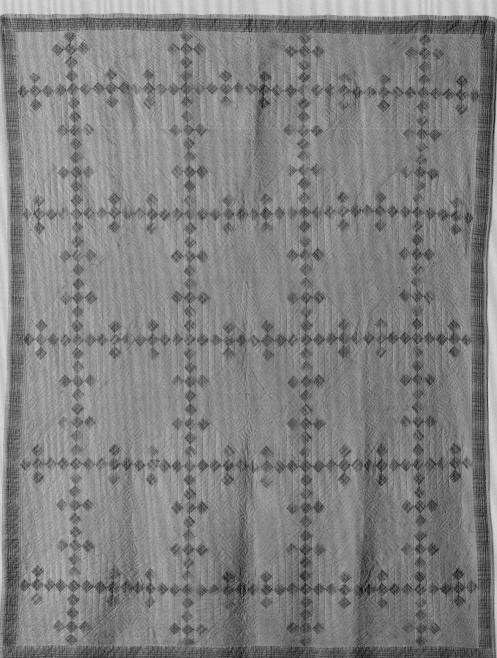

MY INSPIRATION

ABOVE Because it uses only two fabrics, this antique quilt didn't grab my attention initially. But what a fun layout it turned out to be for us! I can now see that it is quite clever how those dark squares float in that cream space. And the quilting really shows up for a change – it's so often lost on my densely patterned quilts. Part of the V&A collection, this quilt was made in the late nineteenth century by Mrs Margaret Whitacre of Montpelier, Indiana, who quilted it beautifully with repeating blocks of overlapping wine-glass circles.

SPRING DOUBLE NINE-PATCH

RIGHT AND BELOW At first I wasn't going to include this very simple quilt format, but when I started applying colours to it I got really excited. On the *Spring Double Nine-Patch Quilt* I've used my lime-toned *Paperweight* print for the background and added accents of bright pastel. The lime is a very committed choice that some will love and others hate. Combined with the same bright pastel accents, the Pastel colourway of my *Paperweight* fabric would make a frothy, more delicate composition, while maintaining the lively dottiness. (See pages 94 and 95 for the instructions.)

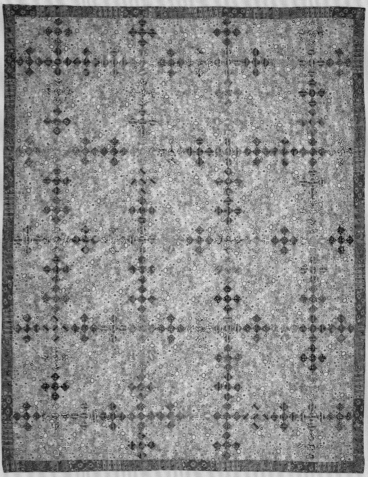

WINTER DOUBLE NINE-PATCH

LEFT AND ABOVE For this darker version of the *Double Nine-Patch*, I used a dark colourway of my *Peony* print called 'Kimono', with its deep plum ground. The accent colours are my *Shot Cottons* and appear like jewels floating on this flower bed. It has a Tibetan mood. If you like this dark mood, but want a tighter small-scale print as the all-over base colour, I suggest using the Gypsy colourway of my *Paperweight* print or Jungle *Roman Glass*. Stitching the one hundred small nine-patch blocks needed for this quilt in one of these varied palettes is a lot more entertaining than repeating the simple two-colour blocks in the V&A original would be. (See pages 94 and 95 for the instructions.)

MY INSPIRATION

ABOVE AND LEFT When I first went to the V&A in the 60s, this 1730 bed hanging was the first patchwork that really caught my attention. It hung in the Textile Galleries and I used to stare at it for hours on my frequent visits. The brilliant mirror imaging of patches inside the diamond blocks makes it surprisingly dynamic. It has the same fascination that a kaleidoscope has with its compelling pattern repetition. The strong, simple Indian prints and the use of darks fans as accents create such a dramatic effect; simple two-colour brocades like this are very fashionable in the textile world just now. Most of the prints have white or off-white grounds, making for a very fresh airy feel. The moss green ribbon provides a perfect framing for the diamond blocks.

PAGES 44 AND 45 The *Clamshell Quilt* shot in a lime-coloured tree, which emphasizes its pink tones.

CLAMSHELL QUILT

ABOVE AND RIGHT The *Clamshell Quilt*, my
interpretation of the V&A original, is a delight
to make if you like hand stitching. I worked
on it with a student helper and the two of
us achieved a finished quilt top but a little
below most quilters' standards. The quilter
did a miraculous job of ironing out our kinks.
Working out all those mirror-image patch
arrangements is a delight that I leave to you
to explore yourself. The quilt is made up
entirely of my own patchwork fabrics —
some designed specially for this book and
inspired by the prints in the old V&A quilts.
(See page 96 for the instructions.)

SQUARE CLAMSHELL QUILT

LEFT AND RIGHT Because the traditional
curving clamshell patch has to be stitched by
hand and some will find it a bit time-
consuming, I designed this squares version as
an alternative to the *Clamshell Quilt* on page
47. It contains the same rhythmic mirror-
image patch arrangements and is made
entirely in my own up-to-date fabrics. Best of
all, it can be made with a sewing machine. I
added pink sashing and inner border to this
version and an outer border of spicy red
leaves. My *Zinnia* print with lime on a bright
orange ground makes an opulent backing for
the quilt. Be sure to choose your backing
fabrics with as much care as you do the quilt
top patch materials. (See pages 97–99 for
the instructions.)

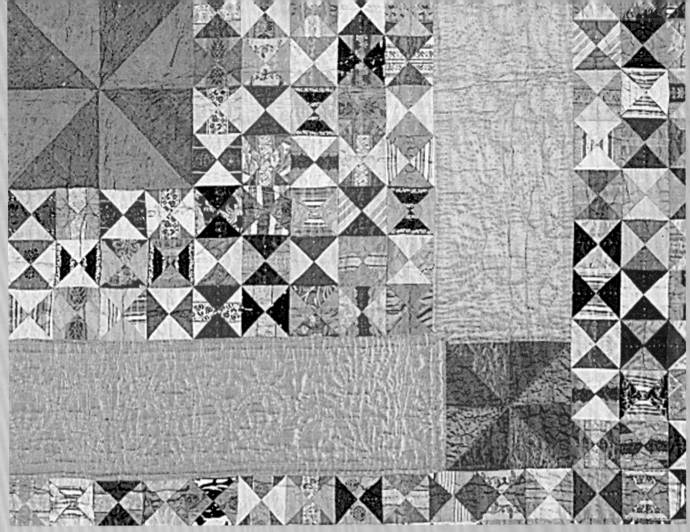

MY INSPIRATION

Liza first spotted this
eighteenth-century V&A patchwork on the
internet after we had started work on this
book. We were both struck by the power of
this simple geometric quilt. On the internet
the colours appeared to be very earthy
browns in tone, hence our interpretation.
Imagine our shock and surprise when we
went to view the quilt in the flesh in the V&A
archive and saw how fresh in colouring it
actually was. Deep pinks and lime greens with
sky blues. What a thrill. We didn't have time
to do a new version for the book, so I leave
it to you to study the close-up shot and
choose fabrics. Good luck!

Pages 50 and 51: My Hourglass Quilt draped
over a red leather sofa in a grand house
in London.

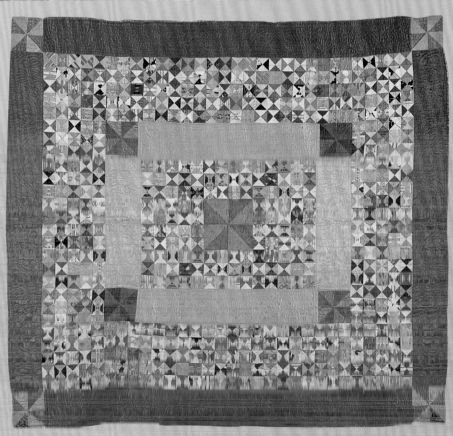

HOURGLASS QUILT

RIGHT An amazingly powerful effect is achieved with simple hourglass blocks and massive borders. I love the colouring of the original. It is like patchwork costumes of the old Commedia dell' Arte. Lime green, chartreuse yellow, terracotta pink and sky blue make for a a joyous palette, indeed. Because we got a more earthy impression from the reproduction on the internet, we did ours in these oranges, browns, rusts and teal blues that make a fine quilt but quite a different mood. (See pages 100–102 for the instructions.)

SHOWPIECE QUILTS

The quilts in this chapter form an extravagant collection. *Mariner's Compass* and *Chequerboard*,
take straightforward geometric forms and repeat them in clever paisley fabrics,
mesmerizing the eye (see pages 63 and 67). The other showpieces in this chapter use
appliqué and curves to create their specialness.

When I first became involved with patchwork I thought it was all about recycling old
garments and furnishing fabrics, but I soon learned that many quilts were made of the finest
materials the sewer could afford to purchase. They used expensive silk ribbon, velvet and
brocade, and sometimes even embroidered this with silk thread and beads. The quilts were
lovingly constructed to be the most extravagant item in the bedroom or sitting room. These
are wonderful in their way, but the use of masses of sample prints brought together in
harmonious combinations is what never fails to amaze me. Our last quilt – the *Sampler
Quilt* – is one of the finest and most intriguing examples of this that I've ever come
across. The more you see it the more you find to wonder at.

LEFT AND ABOVE The Rembrandt browns of this painted tapestry and the black-and-white stone floor are a rich
backdrop for my *Chequerboard Quilt* (see page 67).

MY INSPIRATION

RIGHT What a witty, amusing combination
of florals, dots and stripes! The use of high
contrast gives clarity to the geometric
patchwork pattern, while allowing a
playful mix of strong prints in a mostly
warm brown, red and cream palette, with
cool blue accents. When I wrote *Glorious
Colour* in 1988, I included this stunning
quilt as an inspiration for designing with
squares and circles. Made by Elizabeth
Chapman in 1829 to celebrate a wedding
in the family, the patchwork was kept as a
cherished item by Chapman descendants
for several generations until it was finally
donated to the V&A. Never finished, it is
unlined and still has basting threads and
printed and hand-written paper templates
on the back. The centrepiece is a block
printed floral panel commemorating the
Duke of Wellington's victory at the Battle
of Vitoria in 1813.

JOCKEY'S CAP BABY QUILT

ABOVE AND RIGHT Made up of contemporary
fabric prints similar to those of the V&A
inspiration, this quilt is very close in colour
mood to its antique source. As the palette is
an unusual and sophisticated one for a child's
quilt and as it is much smaller than the
original, it would make a fabulous wall
hanging, too. For the quilt centre, I designed
the pot of flowers to update the printed
floral centrepiece of the original. The
lollipop flowers appliquéd to form the small
jockey cap blocks. A less contrasting, delicate
pastel interpretation of this format would be
charming. (See pages 103 and 104 for the
instructions.)

PAGES 58 AND 59 The Victorian rocking
horse, with its grey markings, seems just the
right setting for a Victorian childhood, and
the *Jockey's Cap Baby Quilt* doesn't look out
of place at all.

FOLK ART QUILT

LEFT AND TOP RIGHT For my adaptation of the antique original of this quilt, I placed the shapes on two tones of my *Peony* print and Liza sewed them on wonderfully. We used an interesting paisley-type stripe for the border, which provides a strong dramatic finish. The echo quilting is deliciously obsessive, the way I enjoy it most. The white-and-blue circles print on a maroon ground, used for the doll shapes, is one of my favourite fabrics in this quilt. It was cut from a shirt I'd had since 1970, which was bought by a friend in a California charity shop. So the quilt contains a lovely memory, as every patchwork should. (See pages 105–107 for the instructions.)

MY INSPIRATION

RIGHT Of all the quilts in the V&A collection, the one that inspired my version here is perhaps the most eccentric and original. It makes me smile every time I see it. The maker had a delicious sense of humour and delight, and the wonderful selection of bold prints used for the silhouetted creatures and objects is awe-inspiring. Matisse himself would bow to this artistry and wit. There doesn't seem to be a story told or a rhyme or reason to the collection of objects the maker chose to feature. Written about by Averil Colby, this appliqué coverlet is attributed to the late nineteenth century.

MY INSPIRATION

LEFT AND ABOVE There are many things to admire about this grand English V&A quilt, made in about 1830. The all-over dance of burnt red, creams, faded blues and a multitude of wood tones give it a marquetry feel. Two outstanding elements are the paisley-stripe triangles almost merging with another brown print, and the next two borders melting together geometrically. The broken dishes border next to the steeple-chase, or jockey's cap, makes a great pair that work a treat together. It is said that there was a passion for closely patterned and coloured textiles in the second quarter of the nineteenth century. I feel the same way in the first half of this century. The thing I love so much about this quilt is how the maker managed such a unified harmony using so many different patterned fabrics. It is this example of melting and merging that inspires my approach to patchwork.

MARINER'S COMPASS QUILT

LEFT AND BELOW As you can see, we hunted high and low to find fabrics similar to those of the original for my *Mariner's Compass Quilt*. It is unusual for me to experience this brown world that many quilters seem to favour. At first glance this version may look like a reproduction, but it is made with anything we could find instead of carefully sourced authentic reproduction period prints. The wonderful multitude of geometric borders is enthralling – rich border piled on rich border like a Bach fugue, working outwards from the central compass. This quilt was assembled in the old-fashioned quilting-bee way. Working in a wonderful shop in Berkeley Heights, New Jersey, the owner, employees, and quilt instructors turned up on their day off to sew the blocks, so we were able to complete this very complex cover much quicker than usual. These women mostly have jobs outside of the shop and also work there to support their fabric habit and to indulge their passion for quilt making. (See pages 108–111 for the instructions.)

MY INSPIRATION

BELOW The most extraordinary quilt in the V&A collection is called King George III Reviewing the Volunteers. It was made in about 1805 and is composed of over 280 miniature pieced rosettes (see below). The rows of rosettes surround a large centrepiece depicting King George on horseback before the troops, with a hilltop village in the background. The wide outer border contains large ovals filled with detailed embroidered and appliquéd historical and domestic scenes. Two of four large circles that border the centrepiece were adapted for the *Sun and Moon Cushions*.

SUN AND MOON CUSHIONS

ABOVE The *Sun Cushion*, an homage to the V&A's most extraordinary quilt, uses a palette much like the sun in the original. I painted the face with acrylic, but you could use fabric paints or pens, or even embroider the features as they were on the V&A source. (See pages 112 and 113 for the instructions.)

RIGHT This bold and vibrant target-like layout could be done in many different fabric moods. Its graphic appearance would stand out impressively in a contemporary interior. So many more cushion ideas could be taken from this amazing King George quilt, if intricate piecing is your bag and you enjoy a series of repeated patterns as a group. (See pages 112 and 113 for the instructions.)

MY INSPIRATION

ABOVE AND LEFT The exciting first impression of this early-nineteenth-century English V&A quilt is the bold all over chequerboard effect of the structure. Then one zeros in on the various scales of pieced chequerboards, from minute one-half-inch squares to more manageable-size ones. The use of paisley prints that are similar in texture to chequerboards and the various fancy stripes is inspired. The warm palette of browns, creams and rusts puts one in mind of a tile floor. Lightening the predominantly brown palette is a lovely touch of soft green and grey blue.

CHEQUERBOARD QUILT

ABOVE AND LEFT On first seeing the intricately pieced V&A original, I must admit I couldn't imagine being able to achieve anything close. There isn't much that can equal the wonderful obsessiveness of this medieval tile floor of a quilt! Still, I have had a go on my *Chequerboard Quilt* at simplifying some of those impossibly minute chequerboards – replacing some with chequerboard-looking prints. I heightened and deepened the rust brown palette and brought in more toasty pink and gold tones. A lot of my own fabric prints are included, such as the *Ikat Chequerboards* and the central *Wild Rose* print. My little *Pansy* prints provide good replacements for the fine pieced chequerboard blocks of the original. (See pages 114–116 for the instructions.)

MY INSPIRATION

ABOVE Probably the most well-known quilt in the V&A's collection is this patchwork, known as the Coverlet. Apparently because it was made in 1797, it is very good condition and was a thrill to see close up in the V&A storage area that I was privileged to. In a phrase, this has to be someone's obsessive life's work — Liza thinks a Bea-Maach aunt, perhaps. I mean, wow, look at those intricate pieced bits of patterned

fabric and the endless variations on the block! There is enough detail here to inspire and interpret for several lifetimes' work!

SAMPLER QUILT

ABOVE It was wonderful to study the great printed cottons on the original quilt, but we had to simplify a lot to adapt it to a contemporary patchwork. The repetition of the rounded shapes helps to hold the disparate parts of the quilt together. Each quarter of the quilt is the same, as on the *Sundial Coverlet*, another unifying design feature. But the thing that really holds all this pattern together, for me,

is the palette. I thought of jewel mosaic bits dropped into a sandy base. So the taupe and grey tones throughout hold the contrasting brighter colours together. (See pages 117–121 for the instructions.)

PAGES 70 AND 71 Details from the *Sampler Quilt*, which was cut entirely from my own fabric designs.

MAKING THE QUILTS

This chapter contains full instructions for each of the patchworks in the book – a
total of 21 quilts and two cushions. Coloured assembly diagrams are given for most of the
quilts, as well as block construction illustrations.

The instructions are cross-referenced with the quilt photographs in the first
three chapters. Be sure to refer to these large photographs when making a quilt, so you
have a better view of the fabrics and colour schemes.

If you are new to patchwork, read the techniques chapter (pages 122–132)
before attempting to make any of the following quilts. Even experienced patchworkers may
find a few helpful tips there.

LEFT AND ABOVE The *Leafy Snowball Quilt* (see page 30 and pages 82 and 83).

FLORAL COLUMNS QUILTS (pages 11–13)

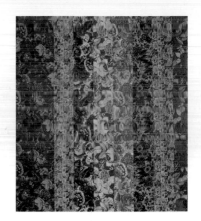

The *Floral Columns Quilts* were inspired by the backing of a crazy patchwork quilt in the V&A. The backing is made of long bold swaths of dramatic leafy prints (see page 10) that are not matched in any way, but the colours are harmonious. The *Dark Floral Columns Quilt* is shown right and on page 11. See page 13 for the *Light Floral Columns Quilt*. Either of these interpretations of the original can be stitched in just a few days.

SIZES OF PATCHWORKS
The finished *Dark Floral Columns [Light Floral Columns]* measures approximately 74¼in x 82½in (189cm x 210cm) [78in x 78in (195cm x 198cm)]

Note: The instructions for the narrower *Dark Floral Columns* are given first and those for *Light Floral Columns* follow in brackets [ ].

MATERIALS
Use 44–45in (112–114cm) wide cotton quilting fabrics

DARK FLORAL COLUMNS
Patchwork fabrics: ½yd (46cm) each of nine different large-scale prints in a deep Victorian palette, including golds, plums, reds, magentas, deep greens and browns

REMAINING INGREDIENTS
Backing fabric: 5yd (4.6m) of desired fabric (choose a fabric that suits the quilt top)

Binding fabric: ¾yd (70cm) of a 'toile' print (KAFFE FASSETT *Fruit Basket Toile* in Teal was used here)
Cotton batting: 82in x 90in (207cm x 228cm)
Quilting thread: Taupe thread

LIGHT FLORAL COLUMNS
Patchwork fabrics: ½yd (46cm) each of 13 different large-scale prints in off-beat pastels, including lavenders, pinks, sky blues, sage, chartreuse, aqua and ecrus

REMAINING INGREDIENTS
Backing fabric: 5yd (4.6m) of desired fabric
Binding fabric: ¾yd (70cm) of a blue ombré stripe (KAFFE FASSETT *Ombré Stripe* in Blue was used here)
Cotton batting: 85in x 85in (213cm x 216cm)
Quilting thread: Ecru thread

CUT PATCHES
Cut two strips 8¾in (22.5cm) [6½in (16.5cm)] wide from each of the 9 [13] different pieces of fabric, cutting from selvedge to selvedge for 18 [26] strips about 44–45in (112–114cm) long. Trim off the selvedge from each end of each strip.

MAKE PATCHWORK STRIPS
Using a ¼in (7.5mm) seam allowance throughout, sew the two pieces of each of the 9 [13] fabrics together end to end.

Then cut each joined strip into two pieces, cutting in a different position on each one. Move the cut-off piece to the opposite end and sew back on. (This is done so that the seams will be in different positions on each strip and to prevent them from all lining up across the middle of the quilt.) Press the seams open.

Trim each of the 9 [13] joined strips to 83in (211.5cm) [78½in (199.5cm)].

ASSEMBLE TOP
Arrange the 9 [13] joined strips side by side, either on the floor or on a cotton-flannel design wall.

Once you have achieved the desired effect, sew the strips together using a ¼in (7.5mm) seam allowance.

FINISH QUILT
Press the quilt top. Layer the quilt top, batting and backing; and baste (see page 131).

Using a taupe [ecru] thread, quilt large leafy shapes [double free form zigzags] down each column.

Trim the quilt edges. Then cut the binding fabric on the bias and attach (see pages 131 and 132).

WELSH QUILT (page 17)

The antique V&A version of the *Welsh Quilt* (see page 16), contains starkly contrasting colours. The aged patina of the fabrics allows the disparate colours to harmonize beautifully. It was a difficult colour combination to bring together with contemporary fabrics. Fresh, unaged fabrics in similar colours created contrasts that appeared too harsh, so this version is coloured slightly differently to retain the feel of the now 'antiqued' original.

This quilt is made entirely of Kaffe Fassett patchwork fabrics. If you want to use your own choices of fabric, pay attention to the tones of the prints, using dark, medium and light tones to create the required contrasts between adjacent patches.

SIZE OF PATCHWORK
The finished *Welsh Quilt* measures approximately 84in x 96in (213.5cm x 244cm).

MATERIALS
Use 44–45in (112–114cm) wide cotton quilting fabrics
Patch and border fabrics: 14 KAFFE FASSETT fabrics as follows –

- ¼yd (25cm) of *Ikat Wash* in Peach
- ½yd (46cm) each of *Lotus* in Ochre and in Red; *Pansy* in Brown; *Zinnia* in Magenta; *Wild Rose* in Lavender and in Ochre; and *Awning Stripe* in Mauve/Sage
- ¾yd (70cm) each of *Wild Rose* in Pastel; *Leaves* in Gold; *Zinnia* in Antique; and *Diagonal Poppy* in Aubergine
- 1yd (92cm) of *Paisley Stripes* in Antique
- 2¼yd (2.1m) of *Ikat Wash* in Banana

REMAINING INGREDIENTS
Backing fabric: 6yd (5.5m) of desired fabric
Binding fabric: ¾yd (70cm) of KAFFE FASSETT *Awning Stripe* in Mauve/Sage
Cotton batting: 91in x 103in (231cm x 262cm)
Quilting thread: Neutral-coloured thread

CUT PATCHES
Note that the triangle patches are all cut from squares. When cutting the triangles, start by cutting each square with the sides carefully aligned with the straight grain of the fabric. Then cut the square in half or in quarters as instructed. For two half-square triangles, cut diagonally from corner to corner. For four quarter-square triangles, cut diagonally from corner to corner in both directions.

The patches are carefully planned so that biased edges can usually be matched to straight-grain edges when they are pieced together. While cutting, you will notice that on each half-square triangle the two short sides are aligned with the straight grain of the fabric; and on each quarter-square triangle the one long side is aligned with the straight grain of the fabric.

QUILT CENTRE
The pieces are cut starting at the centre of the quilt. Keep the patches organized, pinning together the patches for each section (or stitching together the sections as they are cut).

Centre diamond: From Ochre *Lotus*, cut one 17⅜in (44cm) square.
4 centre border strips: From Peach *Ikat Wash*, cut four strips 3⅜in x 17⅜in (8.5cm x 44cm).
4 centre-border squares: From Magenta *Zinnia*, cut four 3⅜in (8.5cm) squares, 'fussy' cutting so that a blossom is centred in each square.
4 large triangles: From Lavender *Wild Rose*, cut two 16⅞in (43cm) squares, then cut each square in half to make a total of four large half-square triangles.

BORDER NO. 1
4 border strips: From Antique *Paisley Stripes*, cut four strips 4⅝in x 32½in (11.5cm x 82.5cm).
4 border squares: From Brown *Pansy*, cut four 4⅝in (11.5cm) squares.

BORDER NO. 2 – SIDES
10 inner triangles: From Pastel *Wild Rose*, cut three 9¼in (23.5cm) squares, then cut each square in quarters to make

a total of 12 quarter-square triangles – only 10 are used.

10 outer triangles: From Antique *Paisley Stripes*, cut five 6⅝in (16.8cm) squares, then cut each square in half to make a total of 10 half-square triangles.

8 squares: Cut four 6¼in (16cm) squares from Brown *Pansy* and four from Magenta *Zinnia*.

4 end-triangles: From Gold *Leaves*, cut one 9¼in (23.5cm) square, then cut in quarters to make a total of four quarter-square triangles.

BORDER NO. 2 – TOP AND BOTTOM

8 inner triangles: From Pastel *Wild Rose*, cut two 11¼in (28.6cm) squares, then cut each square in quarters to make a total of eight quarter-square triangles.

8 outer triangles: From Antique *Paisley Stripes*, cut four 7⅞in (20cm) squares, then cut each square in half to make a total of eight half-square triangles.

6 squares: From Ochre *Wild Rose*, cut six 7½in (19cm) squares.

4 end-triangles: From Ochre *Wild Rose*, cut one 11¼in (28.6cm) square, then cut in quarters to make a total of four quarter-square triangles.

4 big rectangles: From Antique *Zinnia*, cut four 8½in x 10½in (21.6cm x 26.7cm) rectangles. (**Note:** Cut patches in Antique *Zinnia* for border no. 4 before cutting these big rectangles.)

BORDER NO. 3

16 inner triangles: From Aubergine *Diagonal Poppy*, cut four 11¼in (28.6cm) squares, then cut each square in quarters to make a total of 16 quarter-square triangles.

12 outer triangles: From Mauve/Sage *Awning Stripe*, cut six 7⅞in (20cm) squares, then cut each square in half to make a total of 12 half-square triangles.

8 end-triangles: From Mauve/Sage *Awning Stripe*, cut two 8¼in (21cm) squares, then cut each square in quarters to make a total of eight quarter-square triangles.

4 side-border rectangles: From Gold *Leaves*, cut four 5½in x 10½in (14cm x 26.7cm) rectangles.

4 top- and bottom-border rectangles: From Gold *Leaves*, cut four 5½in x 8½in (14cm x 21.6cm) rectangles.

4 top- and bottom-border squares: From Magenta *Zinnia*, cut four 5½in (14cm) squares.

BORDER NO. 4 (ONE STRIP ONLY)

4 inner triangles: From Red *Lotus*, cut one 17¾in (45cm) square, then cut in quarters to make a total of four quarter-square triangles.

3 outer triangles: From Antique *Zinnia*, cut one 17¾in (45cm) square, then cut in quarters to make a total of four quarter-square triangles – only three are used.

2 end-triangles: From Antique *Zinnia*, cut one 9⅛in (23.2cm) square, then cut in half to make a total of two half-square triangles.

BORDER NO. 5

4 squares: From Gold *Leaves*, cut four 9½in (24cm) squares

4 strips: From Banana *Ikat Wash*, cut eight strips 9½in (24cm) wide, cutting from selvedge to selvedge. Cut off the selvedges and sew the strips together end to end to make a continuous strip. Then, from this strip, cut two side-border strips each 78½in (199.4cm) long, and a top-border strip and a bottom-border strip each 66½in (169cm) long.

ASSEMBLE TOP

Sew the quilt pieces together as described below, using a ¼in (6mm) seam allowance throughout. Be sure to stitch bias edges carefully; when sewing a straight-grain edge to a bias edge, place the bias edge against the sewing machine feed dogs (the 'teeth') to help ease them together.

Assemble the quilt from the centre outwards. Following the diagram (see below), sew two centre-border strips to opposite sides of the big centre diamond. Then sew a centre-border square to each end of each of the remaining two centre-border strips and sew these strips in place. Join on the four large triangles to complete the quilt centre. Follow the diagram (see next page) to piece together and

Assembly – centre square of Welsh Quilt

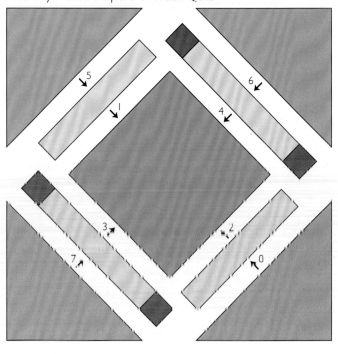

join on the borders. Attach the side strips of each border first, as shown, followed by the top and bottom strips.

FINISH QUILT
Press the quilt top. Layer the quilt top, batting and backing; and baste (see page 131).

Using a neutral-coloured thread, quilt clamshell shapes in the centre, quilt meandering lines in some borders, and stitch concentric semi-circles in some triangles. Quilt the outside border with traditional 'Baptist fans'.

Trim the quilt edges. Then cut the binding fabric on the bias and attach (see pages 131 and 132).

Assembly – borders of Welsh Quilt

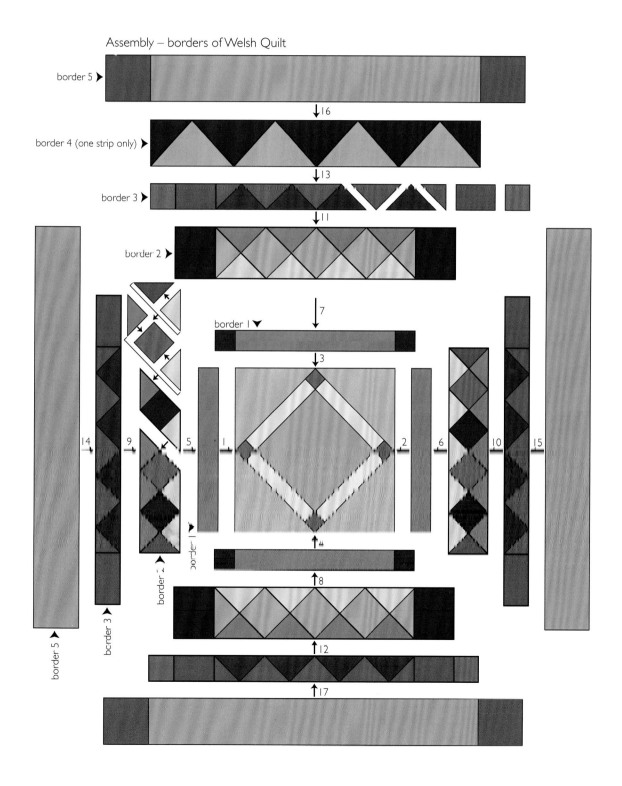

SARAH'S PATCHWORKS (pages 21–23)

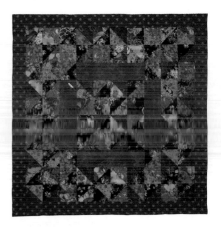

The inspiration quilt for these two easy-to-make patchworks is English and was made by Sarah Wyatt in 1801 (see page 20). They are 'one patch' quilts; in other words, a single patch is used to make the entire quilt, except for the inner and outer borders. Using a single patch is very handy because you can adjust the size of the quilt quite easily, just as we have done here. The original quilt is bed sized and our *Pastel* version is a little larger to fit today's beds (see page 21). The *Gypsy* colourway is made up of smaller triangles for a throw-size patchwork (see right and page 22).

SIZES OF PATCHWORKS

The finished *Sarah's Gypsy Throw [Sarah's Pastel Quilt]* measures approximately 69in x 69in (175cm x 175cm) [92in x 92in (91cm x 122cm)].

Note: The instructions for the smaller *Sarah's Gypsy Throw* are given first and those for *Sarah's Pastel Quilt* follow in [ ].

MATERIALS

Use 44–45in (112–114cm) wide cotton quilting fabrics

SARAH'S GYPSY THROW

PATCHWORK BLOCK FABRICS

Fabric A: ¼–½yd (25–46cm) each of assortment of florals with black and/or dark brown backgrounds; at least 2yd (1.8m) total

Fabric B: ¼–½yd (25–46cm) each of assortment of medium-toned mostly gold florals and/or paisleys; at least 2yd (1.8m) total

Fabric C: ¼–½yd (25–46cm) each of assortment of deep-toned large-scale florals with black and/or paisleys in magentas, reds, deep blues, deep greens and purples; at least 4yd (3.6m) total

BORDER FABRICS

Inner border: ¾yd (70cm) of KAFFE FASSETT *Fruit Basket Toile* in Red or a similar 'toile' print

Outer border: 2yd (1.9m) of KAFFE FASSETT *Ikat Dot* in Scarlet or a similar polka dot fabric

REMAINING INGREDIENTS

Backing fabric: 4½yd (4.2m) of desired fabric

Binding fabric: ¾yd (70cm) of a stripe (KAFFE FASSETT *Narrow Stripe* 09 was used here)

Cotton batting: 76in (193cm) square

Quilting thread: Deep red thread

SARAH'S PASTEL QUILT

PATCHWORK BLOCK FABRICS

Fabric A: 1yd (92cm) each of at least three pink 'toile' prints

Fabric B: ¼–½yd (25–46cm) each of assortment of fabrics in light-toned taupe, periwinkle, grey, blue, ochre-coloured spots fabrics, soft-coloured stripes, pale florals, mosaic-type patterns in blue, pink and grey; at least 9yd (8.3m) total

BORDER FABRICS

Inner and outer borders: 2¾yd (2.5m) of KAFFE FASSETT *Fruit Basket Toile* in Pink or a similar deep pink on off-white 'toile' print

REMAINING INGREDIENTS

Backing fabric: 7yd (6.4m) of desired fabric

Binding fabric: ¾yd (70cm) of KAFFE FASSETT *Kashmir* in Pink

Cotton batting: 99in (252cm) square

Quilting thread: Pale pink thread

CUT PATCHES

Cut the borders first, then cut the triangle patches.

BORDERS

Outer borders: From the outer border fabric, cut two strips 5in x 60½in (13cm x 154cm) [6½in x 80½in (16.5cm x 204cm)] and two strips 5in x 69½in (13cm x 177cm) [6½in x 92½in (16.5cm x 235.5cm)]. (See Materials above for which fabric to use for the two versions of the quilt.)

Inner borders: From the inner border fabric, cut four strips 6½in x 24½in (16.5cm x 62.5cm) [8½in x 32½in (21.5cm x 82.5cm)].

PATCHWORK BLOCKS

168 triangles: Cut at least eighty-four 6⅞in (17.5cm) [8⅞in (22.5cm)] squares from an assortment of all the fabrics, except the border fabrics for the *Gypsy Throw* version. Then cut the squares from corner to corner for the 168 triangles. (When arranging the quilt, you will see that it helps to develop a good colour balance if you have some extra triangles at hand; so be sure to cut some extras in a range of colours.)

MAKE BLOCKS

Arrange the whole quilt, either on the floor or on a cotton-flannel design wall before making the blocks. *Sarah's Gypsy Throw* is made up of four pinwheel blocks at the centre and 16 diamond blocks around the inner border. Note that there is a fabric-A (black or brown) and fabric-B (gold) diamond in the centre of each block and in the two centre positions in the quilt centre. The fabric C colours appear randomly, but the black or brown should remain consistent.

Sarah's Pastel Quilt is made up entirely of pinwheel blocks (except for the corner blocks in the inner border). The colours are used at random for an overall wash of pale colours and a somewhat haphazard appearance.

16 [0] diamond blocks: Using a ¼in (6mm) seam allowance, make 16 [0] diamond blocks as shown in the diagram (see right).

4 [20] pinwheel blocks: Using a ¼in (6mm) seam allowance, make 4 [20] pinwheel blocks as shown in the diagram (see right).

4 [4] corner blocks: Using a ¼in (6mm) seam allowance, make 4[4] corner blocks as shown in the diagram.

ASSEMBLE TOP

Following the assembly diagram (see right) and using a ¼in (6mm) seam allowance throughout, sew together the two rows of two pinwheel blocks for the quilt centre.

Now sew an inner-border strip to each side of the quilt centre. Then sew a corner block to each end of each of the remaining two strips and sew these to the top and bottom of the quilt centre.

Sew three diamond [pinwheel] blocks together for each side and sew these to the centre. Sew five diamond [pinwheel] blocks together for the top and bottom and sew these in position.

Sew the shorter outer-border strips to the sides of the patchwork and the longer strips to the top and bottom.

FINISH QUILT

Press the quilt top. Layer the quilt top, batting and backing; and baste (see page 131).

Using a deep red [pale pink] thread, quilt concentric fan shapes in the borders and overall scallop shapes in the centre.

Trim the quilt edges. Then cut the binding fabric on the bias and attach (see pages 131 and 132).

FABRIC KEY

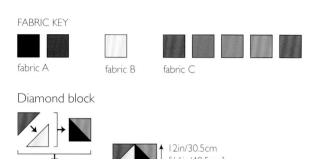

fabric A   fabric B   fabric C

Diamond block

12in/30.5cm [16in/40.5cm] (finished size excluding seam allowances)

Pinwheel block

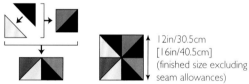

12in/30.5cm [16in/40.5cm] (finished size excluding seam allowances)

Corner blocks

6in/15cm [8in/20cm] (finished size excluding seam allowances)

Assembly – Sarah's Gypsy Throw

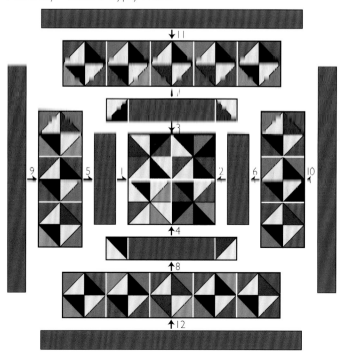

BRICKS PATCHWORKS (pages 25–27)

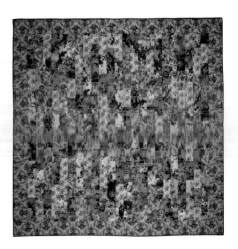

Bricks quilts are true 'utility' quilts. Rectangular patches are cut from a variety of fabrics, not necessarily of a single style or theme, and are sewn together to make a quilt quickly. The aim is to create a warm cover. Sometimes this simple format results in a visual treat, as in the case of the Ufra inspiration (see page 24.)

The larger version, the *Floral Bricks Quilt* (see right) is made up of 'toile' and floral prints, while the *Bricks Baby Quilt* consists of Kaffe Fassett fabrics in a blue-and-white coloration with accents in gold and green (see next page). This format is so simple that you could easily make up your own original version.

SIZES OF PATCHWORKS
The finished *Floral Bricks Quilt [Bricks Baby Quilt]* measures approximately 79in x 80in (200.5cm x 203cm) [42in x 55in (106.5cm x 139.5cm)].
Note: The instructions for the *Floral Bricks Quilt* are given first and those for the *Bricks Baby Quilt* follow in brackets [ ].

MATERIALS
Use 44–45in (112–114cm) wide cotton quilting fabrics

FLORAL BRICKS QUILT
Brick-patch fabrics: ¼–½yd (25–46cm) each of at least 15 different 'toile' prints and medium-scale and large-scale florals, in mostly golds, roses, dusty lavenders, celery, mauves, khakis and peach; at least 6yd (5.5m) total
Border fabric: 1½yd (1.4m) of a gold and rose 'toile' print

REMAINING INGREDIENTS
Backing fabric: 5yd (4.6m) of desired fabric
Binding fabric: ¾yd (70cm) of a rose and gold plaid

Cotton batting: 86in x 87in (219cm x 221cm)
Quilting thread: Neutral pale-coloured thread

BRICKS BABY QUILT
Brick-patch fabrics: Nine KAFFE FASSETT fabrics as follows —
◆ ¼yd (25cm) each of *Peony* in Blue, in Green and in Violet; *Fruit Basket Toile* in Taupe; *Ombré Stripe* in Pink and in Blue; and *Blue-and-White Stripe No. 02*
◆ ½yd (46cm) each of *Organic Stripe* in Blue and in Ochre
Border fabric: ¾yd (70cm) of KAFFE FASSETT *Kashmir* in Aqua

REMAINING INGREDIENTS
Backing fabric: 2yd (1.9m) of desired fabric
Binding fabric: ½yd (46cm) of KAFFE FASSETT *Ombré Stripe* in Blue
Cotton batting: 49in x 62in (125cm x 158cm)
Quilting thread: Pale blue thread

CUT PATCHES
253 [96] brick patches: Cut 253 [96] rectangles each 3½in x 7½in (9cm x 19cm). (Note that the brick patches are the same size for both quilts.)
4 border strips: Cut two side-border strips each 5½in x 70½in (14cm x 179cm) [3½in x 49½in (9cm x 126cm)] and a top- and bottom-border strip each 5½in x 79½in (14cm x 202cm) [3½in x 42½in (9cm x 108cm)]

ASSEMBLE TOP
Arrange the brick patches, either on the floor or on a cotton-flannel design wall. Create 23 [12] narrow vertical

rows of 11 [8] bricks each, placing them end to end. (Note that the brick seams will be staggered, so they will not line up across the quilt.)

Once you have achieved the desired effect, sew together the bricks in each vertical row, using a ¼in (6mm) seam allowance throughout. Press the strips.

Arrange the strips again, positioning the seams in staggered positions. Each of the strips needs to be trimmed to 70½in (179cm) [49½in (126cm)], so mark the trimming position at each end of each strip. Trim the strips to exactly the same length. (Do not be tempted to trim the strips after they are sewn together, as it is too difficult to join the staggered-seam strips flatly if they are different lengths.)

Sew the 23 [12] vertical strips together. Then sew a side-border strip to each side of the quilt. Sew the two remaining border strips to the top and bottom of the quilt.

FINISH QUILT
Press the quilt top. Layer the quilt top, batting and backing; and baste (see page 131).

Using a neutral pale-coloured [pale blue] thread, stitch simple, large 'utility' quilting zigzags over the quilt. (Simple quilting is best so that it doesn't appear fussier than the simple rectangle format.)

Trim the quilt edges. Then cut the binding fabric on the bias and attach (see pages 131 and 132).

LEAFY SNOWBALL QUILT (page 30)

The snowball is a very old traditional patchwork pattern. A charming example of this pattern can be found in the V&A Museum in the form of a set of patchwork seat cushions. The cushions, made by the textile historian Averil Colby in 1953, are black, white and grey (see page 32). The version offered here has been done in a green colourway inspired by the great leafy images found in the V&A's extensive tapestry collection. Some of the Kaffe Fassett fabrics listed in the instructions here are older prints and may be hard to find; however, new large-scale leafy prints are always being added to the collection, and any assortment of mostly green fabrics will work well for this quilt.

SIZE OF PATCHWORK
The finished *Leafy Snowball Quilt* measures approximately 70in x 90in (178cm x 228.5cm).

MATERIALS
Use 44–45in (112–114cm) wide cotton quilting fabrics

PATCHWORK FABRICS
Fabric A: Assortment of KAFFE FASSETT light-toned to medium-toned leafy green prints, with a smattering of reds, greys and golds as follows –
◆ 1yd (92cm) of *Flower Lattice* in Leafy
◆ ¾yd (70cm) each of *Floral Dance* in Pink, *Artichoke* in Leafy, *Roman Glass* in Stone and *Chrysanthemum* in Green
◆ ½yd (46cm) each of *Damask* in Jewel, *Chard* in Leafy, *Floral Lattice* in Pastel and *Dotty* in Seafoam
◆ ¼yd (25cm) each of *Fruit Basket Toile* in Gold, in Teal and in Taupe

Fabric B: Assortment of KAFFE FASSETT dark-medium-toned solid-coloured fabrics in greyed lavenders, ochres, turquoises and grey pink as follows –
◆ ¼yd (25cm) each of *Shot Cotton* in Tobacco, in Forget-me-not, in Jade, in Mushroom, in Lichen, in Slate and in Raspberry

Border fabric: 2¾yd (2.5m) of KAFFE FASSETT *Peony* in Green (leftover fabric after cutting border goes with other fabric-A prints)

REMAINING INGREDIENTS
Backing fabric: 6yd (5.5m) of desired fabric
Binding fabric: ¾yd (70cm) of KAFFE FASSETT *Broad Stripe No. 23*
Cotton batting: 77in x 97in (195cm x 245cm)
Quilting thread: Green thread
Templates: Use templates P and Q (page 134)

CUT PATCHES
Cut the borders first, then cut the patches.
Borders: To make long enough pieces for the border, first cut strips 5½in (14cm) wide from the border fabric, cutting from selvedge to selvedge. Cut off the selvedges and sew the strips together end to end until the continuous strip is at least 282in (717cm) long. Then cut two strips 5½in x 60½in (14cm x 154cm) and two strips 5½in x 80½in (14cm x 204.5cm).
192 big snowball-block squares: Using large square template P, cut a total of 192 squares from the 12 fabric-A prints and the remaining border fabric as follows –
21 Green *Peony* (leftover border fabric); 28 Leafy *Flower Lattice*; 10 Pink *Floral Dance*; 23 Leafy *Artichoke*; 13 Stone *Roman Glass*; 24 Green *Chrysanthemum*; 9 Jewel *Damask*; 19 Leafy *Chard*; 15 Pastel *Floral Lattice*; 13 Seafoam *Dotty*; 7 Gold *Fruit Basket Toile*; 6 Teal *Fruit Basket Toile*; and 4 Taupe *Fruit Basket Toile*.
Small snowball-block corners: Using small square template Q, cut 116 squares from each of the seven fabric-B solid colours for a total of 812 corners; this allows for extras to play with when arranging patches.
4 corner squares: Using square template P, cut four squares from Leafy *Flower Lattice*.

ARRANGE TOP
This quilt must be arranged before making the snowball blocks because the colour on the each corner of each

snowball block must match its neighbour. Arrange the 192 large square patches on the floor or on a cotton-flannel design wall so that there are 16 rows of 12 squares each. Be sure to sprinkle the reds, greys and golds carefully throughout. Once you have achieved the desired effect, make a pile of small squares, taking up to 29 squares from each fabric-B colour. Using these, position a small square at each intersection, sprinkling the colours around for a nice balance.

If you cannot leave the final arrangement in place on the floor or on a cotton-flannel design wall until you have finished sewing the blocks, then draw yourself a 'map' to follow as you sew so that you will know which colour to sew to each corner of each snowball block. This is important if you want the corners to make a solid diamond when sewn together. An occasional error, however, will just add a bit of quirkiness that enhances the liveliness of the patchwork.

MAKE SNOWBALL BLOCKS

Each snowball block is made using one large square and four small squares. Before stitching each block, use a pencil to draw a diagonal line from corner to corner on the wrong side of each of the four small squares.

As shown in the diagram (see below), pin a small square to each corner of the large square with right sides of the fabric together and with the lines on the small squares at an angle across the corners. Align the edges of the fabrics carefully. Sew each small square in place, stitching along the pencil line. Then trim the seam allowances to ¼in (6mm) and press the corners back.

Make all 192 snowball blocks in the same way.

ASSEMBLE TOP

Using the seam allowance marked on template P and following the diagram (see below), sew the snowball blocks together in 16 rows of 12 blocks each. Join the rows together.

Using a ¼in (6mm) seam allowance, sew one long border strip to each side of the quilt. Next, sew a corner square to each end of the two short border strips. Then sew these to the top and bottom of the quilt.

FINISH QUILT

Press the quilt top. Layer the quilt top, batting and backing; and baste (see page 131).

Using a green thread, quilt free-form leafy shapes over the quilt.

Trim the quilt edges. Then cut the binding fabric on the bias and attach (see pages 131 and 132).

FABRIC KEY

fabric A   fabric B   border fabric

Snowball block

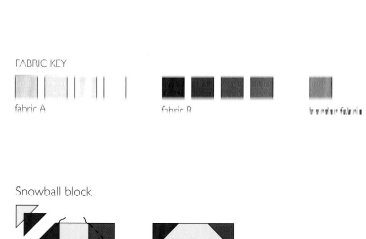

1. Stitch and trim.   2. Press corners back.

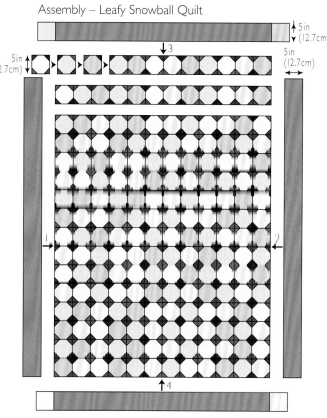

Assembly – Leafy Snowball Quilt

5in (12.7cm)

Note: Measurements on diagram are for finished size, excluding seam allowance.

WEDDING SNOWBALL QUILT

(pages 32 and 33)

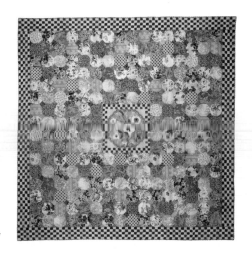

The wonderful V&A wedding quilt that is one of the inspirations for this patchwork has a printed chintz centre medallion surrounded by jockey cap blocks. The *Jockey's Cap Baby Quilt* on page 57 is close in colour and style to the original. We also wanted to make a version that would not be too difficult or time-consuming, so we combined the idea of a central floral panel with snowball blocks. The snowballs are much faster and easier to make than the jockey cap blocks, but the effect is still one of roundness. The addition of unexpected 'off' pastels to the blue-and-white theme gives this quilt the look of beautiful old tiles.

SIZE OF PATCHWORK

The finished *Wedding Snowball Quilt* measures approximately 90in x 90in (228.5cm x 228.5cm).

MATERIALS

Use 44–45in (112–114cm) wide cotton quilting fabrics

PATCHWORK FABRICS

Fabric A: ¼–½yd (25–46cm) each of at least 15–20 different light- to medium-toned, large- or medium-scale blue-and-white prints and monochromatic prints in blues; at least 8yd (7.3m) total
Fabric B: ¼yd (25cm) each of assortment of medium-dark-toned simple small-scale prints, plaids and dots in chartreuse, dull lavenders, ochres, dull apricots, caramels and salmon pink; at least 3yd (2.8m) total
Border fabric: 1¾yd (1.6m) of KAFFE FASSETT *Checkerboard Ikat* in Blue-and-White or a similar check fabric

MEDALLION FABRICS

Background fabric: 20in (51cm) square of a pale aqua fabric

Corner fabric: ¼yd (46cm) of a solid pinkish off-white fabric
Ribbon-edging fabric: ¼yd (46cm) of a simple pink and off-white stripe
Appliqué fabrics: Assortment of scraps of simple prints, solids, monochromatic prints and stripes in various colours (when choosing these fabrics, study the close-up photograph of quilt centre on page 32 and the Fabric Key for the appliqué on page 137)

REMAINING INGREDIENTS

Backing fabric: 9yd (8.3m) of desired fabric
Binding fabric: ¾yd (70cm) of KAFFE FASSETT *Artichoke* in Pastel or a similar print
Cotton batting: 97in x 97in (246cm x 246cm)
Quilting thread: Pale pink thread
Templates: Use snowball templates P and Q (page 134) medallion templates W, X, Y and Z (pages 135 and 136), and appliqué shapes (page 137), enlarging shapes as indicated

MAKE APPLIQUÉ TEMPLATES

Trace the appliqué shapes onto heavy, stiff paper (called card stock) and cut them out. Alternatively, trace the whole appliqué image onto freezer paper and cut out the individual shapes (see page 130).

CUT PATCHES

MEDALLION CENTRE

Background: Using template W, cut medallion background from background fabric.

4 corners: Using template Z, cut four corners from corner fabric.
8 ribbon-edging pieces: From the striped edging fabric, cut four template-X pieces and four template-Y pieces, with the stripe running parallel to the long edges.
Appliqué shapes: Using the templates, lightly trace each of the shapes onto the right side of the appliqué fabrics. (Alternatively, iron the freezer-paper shapes onto the fabrics.) Cut out each of the shapes, cutting ¼in (6mm) from the outer edge for the hem/seam allowance.

FABRIC KEY

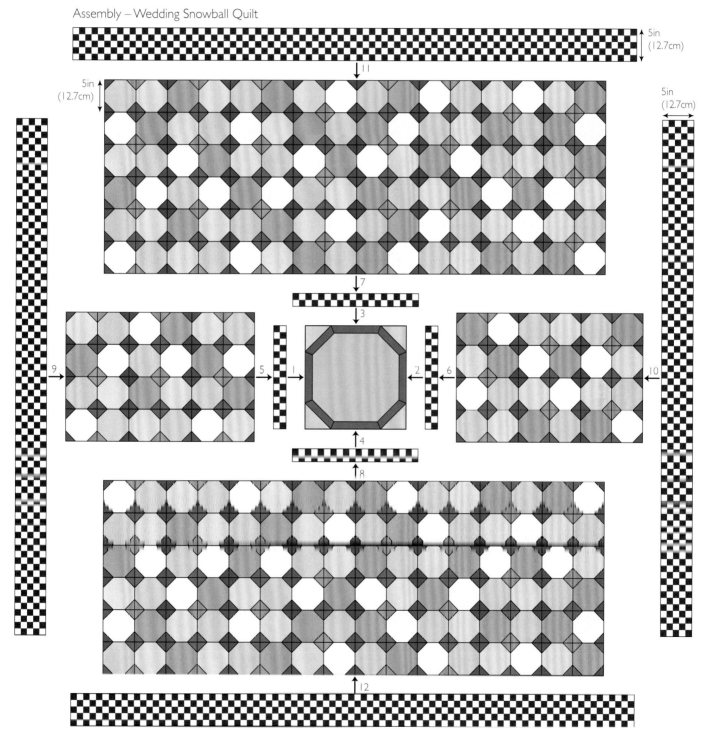

fabric A

fabric B

border fabric

medallion background

medallion edging

medallion corners

Assembly – Wedding Snowball Quilt

5in (12.7cm)

5in (12.7cm)

5in (12.7cm)

Note: Measurements on diagram are for finished size, excluding seam allowance.

SNOWBALL BLOCKS

240 big squares: Using large square template P, cut a total of 240 squares from fabric A.

960 small snowball-block corners: Using small square template Q, cut a total of 960 squares from fabric B, cutting in sets of four matching squares.

BORDERS

Outer border: To make long enough pieces for the outer border, first cut strips 5½in (14cm) wide from the border fabric, cutting from selvedge to selvedge. Cut off the selvedges and sew the strips together end to end until the continuous strip is at least 345in (880cm) long. Then cut two outer-border strips 5½in x 80½in (14cm x 204.5cm) and two strips 5½in x 90½in (14cm x 230cm).

Inner border: To fit around the central medallion, cut two inner-border strips 2½in x 20½in (6.5cm x 52cm) and two strips 2½in x 16½in (6.5cm x 42cm).

SEW APPLIQUÉD CENTRE

Using the seam allowance marked on the templates, sew the four template-X pieces and four template-Y ribbon-edging pieces to the medallion background, then join them at the places where they meet. Sew the corners to the template-X edging pieces.

Prepare the appliqué pieces, stitching them together using your preferred appliqué method (see page 130).

With the right side facing upwards, pin the prepared appliqué to the right side of the pieced background. Slip stitch the appliqué in place using fine thread and remove the basting. Then cut away the background fabric behind the appliqué to within about ¼in (6mm) of the slip stitching, so the background colour will not show through.

Press the finished appliquéd centre.

Sew one shorter inner-border strip to each side of the medallion, then sew the longer strips to the top and bottom. It is not important for the checks on the print to match exactly.

ARRANGE TOP

This quilt must be arranged before making the snowball blocks, because the colour on the each corner of each snowball block must match its neighbour. Arrange the 240 large square patches on the floor or on a cotton-flannel design wall so that there are 16 rows of 16 squares each, with a four-by-four section missing in the centre for the medallion. Once you have achieved the desired effect, position a small fabric-B square at each intersection, sprinkling the colours around for a nice balance.

If you cannot leave the final arrangement in place on the floor or on a cotton-flannel design wall until you have

finished sewing the blocks, then draw yourself a 'map' to follow as you sew so that you will know which colour to sew to each corner of each snowball block. This is important if you want the corners to make a solid diamond when sewn together.

MAKE SNOWBALL BLOCKS

Each snowball block is made using one large square and four small squares. Before stitching each block, draw a line from corner to corner on the wrong side of the four small squares.

As shown in the snowball block diagram (see page 83), pin a small square to each corner of the large square with right sides of the fabric together and with the lines on the small squares at an angle across the corners. Align the edges of the fabrics carefully. Sew each small square in place, stitching along the pencil line. Then trim the seam allowances to ¼in (6mm) and press the corners back.

Make all 240 snowball blocks in the same way.

ASSEMBLE TOP

Using the seam allowance marked on template P, sew the snowball blocks together in four panels as shown on the assembly diagram — two panels for the sides that are each six snowballs by four, and two for the top and bottom that are each 16 snowballs by six. When making the panels, join the blocks together in rows, then join the rows together.

Using a ¼in (6mm) seam allowance, sew one short outer-border strip to each side of the quilt, then sew the longer strips to the top and bottom.

FINISH QUILT

Press the quilt top. Layer the quilt top, batting and backing; and baste (see page 131).

Using a pale pink thread, stitch in-the-ditch around each snowball block and stitch a circle ¼in (6mm) inside each snowball. Stitch around each of the squares on the border fabric. Stitch free-form squiggles on the pinkish off-white medallion corners and the aqua background. Use various thread colours to enhance the appliqué, adding veins in the leaves and detailing the flowers.

Trim the quilt edges. Then cut the binding fabric on the bias and attach (see pages 131 and 132).

PERSIAN-BLUE STARS QUILT (page 35)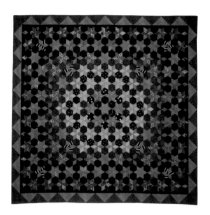

This quilt is very difficult to make by machine because of the large number of inset seams. If you are skilled in accurate cutting and piecing, however, then machine sewing this top is a satisfying way to show off skills. Hand-piecing the quilt centre using the easy English paper-piecing technique is much simpler. The border is easily machine stitched. If you decide to use the English paper-piecing method and require slightly larger seam allowances, be sure to buy a little more fabric than suggested.

SIZE OF PATCHWORK
The finished *Persian Blue Stars Quilt* measures approximately 106in x 100½in (269cm x 255.5cm).

SPECIAL FABRIC NOTE
The quilt centre is made up entirely of diamond patches (AA), except for the two edging pieces (BB and CC). A 2½in (6.4cm) strip of fabric cut from selvedge to selvedge from a 44in (112cm) wide fabric will make 14 diamonds, and ½yd (46cm) will yield 98 diamonds.

The stars alternate with the tumbling-block shapes in concentric rings around the centre block; each star uses either one or two colours and each tumbling block uses one colour. It is best to get enough fabric for an entire ring of stars or tumbling blocks. However, running out of fabric, as we did a few times, is not a disaster and can even add vibrancy. Just make sure that if you do run short of a fabric, you find a very close match in colour (pattern does not matter) so that the change doesn't break up the cohesion of the ring. The fabrics used are mostly solids, monochromatic prints, tie-dye prints and a few polka dots.

MATERIALS
Use 44–45in (112–114cm) wide cotton quilting fabrics

STAR FABRICS
The 15 different star fabrics are all light-medium-toned to dark-medium-toned fabrics –
◆ **Fabric A:** 1¾yd (1.6m) strong turquoise (also used in border)
◆ **Fabric B:** ¼yd (25cm) medium periwinkle
◆ **Fabric C:** 1¼yd (1.2m) second medium periwinkle
◆ **Fabric D:** ¼yd (25cm) turquoise ground with orange dots
◆ **Fabric E:** ¼yd (25cm) medium turquoise
◆ **Fabric F:** ½yd (46cm) second medium turquoise
◆ **Fabric G:** ½yd (46cm) aqua
◆ **Fabric H:** ¼yd (25cm) third medium turquoise

◆ **Fabric I:** ¼yd (25cm) strong magenta
◆ **Fabric J:** ½yd (46cm) medium green ground with purple dots
◆ **Fabric K:** ½yd (46cm) medium blue
◆ **Fabric L:** ¾yd (70cm) turquoise tie-dye print with green and purple accents
◆ **Fabric M:** ½yd (46cm) cobalt blue
◆ **Fabric N:** ¼yd (25cm) ochre
◆ **Fabric O:** ¼yd (25cm) navy and emerald stripe

TUMBLING-BLOCKS FABRICS
The nine tumbling-blocks fabrics are all darker than the star fabrics so that they recede and the stars come forwards –
◆ **Fabric Q:** ¼yd (25cm) navy with fine white stripes
◆ **Fabric R:** ¼yd (25cm) navy ikat with green dots
◆ **Fabric S:** ¼yd (25cm) deep sea green
◆ **Fabric T:** ¼yd (25cm) deep plum
◆ **Fabric U:** ½yd (46cm) navy ground with grey dots
◆ **Fabric V:** ¾yd (70cm) blue ikat with red dots
◆ **Fabric W:** ¾yd (70cm) ochre tie-dye print with orange and red accents
◆ **Fabric X:** 2½yd (2.3m) navy (also used for template BB and template CC edge patches)
◆ **Fabric Y:** 1¾yd (1.6m) sapphire blue

BORDER FABRICS
The outer border is made from the remaining fabric A (see above) and the following –
◆ **Fabric Z:** 2yd (1.9m) deep blue

REMAINING INGREDIENTS
Backing fabric: 9yd (8.3m) of desired fabric
Binding fabric: 1yd (92cm) of a blue dot print (KAFFE FASSETT *Dotty* in Cobalt was used here)
Cotton batting: 113in x 108in (287cm x 275cm)
Quilting thread: Dark navy or black thread
Templates: Use templates AA, BB, CC, DD and EE (pages 138 and 139)

CUT PATCHES

To cut the diamond patches, first cut strips of fabric 2½in (6.4cm) wide, cutting from selvedge to selvedge. Then using template AA, cut each strip into 14 sixty-degree diamonds – each diamond cut in this way will have two sides on the straight grain of the fabric.

Template-AA diamonds: Cut diamonds from the star and tumbling blocks fabric as follows 42 A, 18 B, 222 C, 36 D, 36 E, 60 F, 60 G, 42 H, 42 I, 48 J, 48 K, 122 L, 96 M, 24 N, 24 O, 18 Q, 18 R, 36 S, 36 T, 54 U, 126 V, 120 W, 256 X and 258 Y.

Template-BB and template-CC edge patches: From fabric X, cut 24 template-BB triangles and 28 template-CC patches.

Template-DD border triangles: For the two side borders, cut 18 template-DD triangles from fabric A and 16 from fabric Z.

Template-EE border triangles: For the top and bottom borders, cut 18 template-EE triangles from fabric A and 16 from fabric Z.

4 large corner triangles: From fabric Z, cut two 11½in (29.2cm) squares, then cut each square in half diagonally from corner to corner, to make a total of four large half-square triangles.

MAKE BLOCKS

If possible, when sewing the diamond patches together join a straight-grain edge to a bias edge to help stabilize the shapes.

The star-hexagon blocks are six-sided and are made from 12 diamond patches – six patches for the star and the remaining six background patches are inset between each of the star points. (The background patches form the tumbling-block shapes in the quilt.)

Follow the block-arrangement diagram carefully when choosing the patches for each block (see page 90). Using the seam allowance marked on the templates throughout, make each star-hexagon block as shown in the diagram (see next page). Sew together the six star diamonds first (these are all straight seams). Press the seams open to make the insets easier to work. Then, one by one, inset each of the six background diamonds in the correct position.

When all the star-hexagon blocks are complete, make the half-hexagon blocks for the edges of the quilt.

ASSEMBLE TOP

QUILT CENTRE

Following the diagram very carefully, start with the centre star-hexagon block and attach the six star-hexagon blocks in the ring around it, one at a time (see next page). There are no easy tricks; this has to be done carefully and by

paying attention to the placement of each fabric. Continue adding the star-hexagon blocks in rings around the centre. When the centre star-hexagon blocks are all assembled, sew the half-hexagon blocks in place along the side edges and the template-BB triangles in place along the top and bottom edges.

BORDERS

Note that the completed quilt centre is NOT square. The sides are slightly shorter than the top and bottom. Therefore pay special attention to the difference between templates DD and EE. DD is slightly smaller and should be used for the side borders. EE is for the top and bottom borders.

Sew nine fabric-A template-DD triangles to eight fabric-Z template-DD triangles to make each side border. Sew these borders to the sides of the quilt.

Sew nine fabric-A template-EE triangles to eight fabric-Z template-EE triangles to make the top border. Make a bottom border in the same way. Sew these borders to the top and bottom of the quilt.

Sew a large fabric-Z triangle to each corner. Press and trim each corner square if necessary.

FABRIC KEY

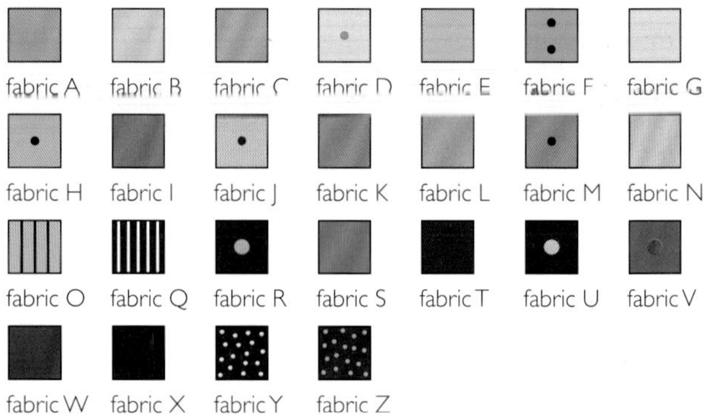

fabric A	fabric B	fabric C	fabric D	fabric E	fabric F	fabric G
fabric H	fabric I	fabric J	fabric K	fabric L	fabric M	fabric N
fabric O	fabric Q	fabric R	fabric S	fabric T	fabric U	fabric V
fabric W	fabric X	fabric Y	fabric Z			

Star hexagon block

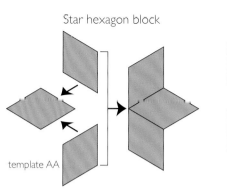

template AA

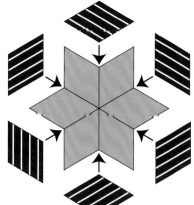

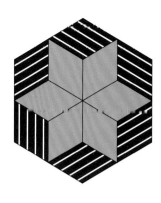

Half-hexagon block

template CC

Assembly — Persian-Blue Stars Quilt

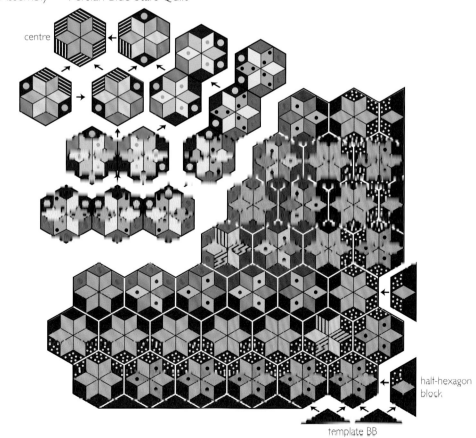

centre

half-hexagon block

template BB

FINISH QUILT

Press the quilt top. Layer the quilt top, batting and backing; and baste (see page 131).

Using dark navy or black thread, machine quilt diagonally through the stars, stitching in-the-ditch and crisscrossing the tumbling blocks. On the border, sew two V-shaped lines about 1in (2.5cm) in from each seam.

Trim the quilt edges. Then cut the binding fabric on the bias and attach (see pages 131 and 132).

Block arrangement — Persian-Blue Stars Quilt

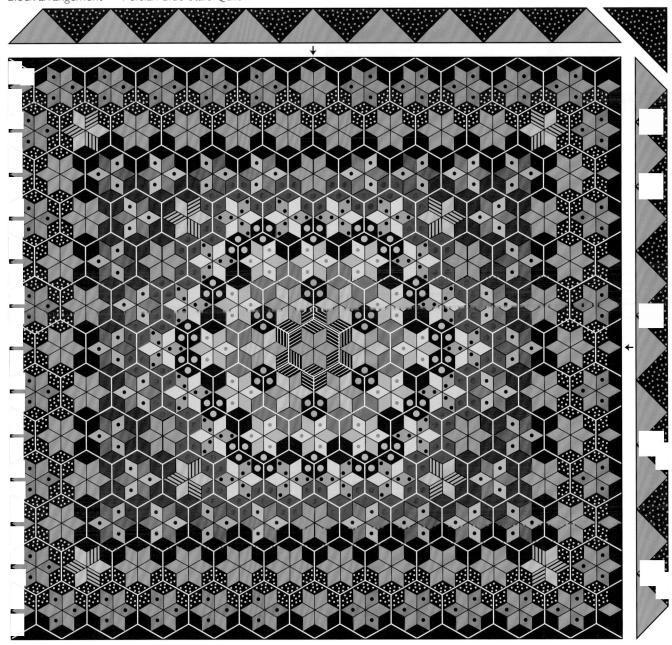

LONE STAR QUILT (page 37)

This version of the V&A's classic lone star patchwork (see page 36) uses striped fabrics in a jazzier way. Instead of the stripes all lining up in the same way, the stripes here face every which way, giving great energy to the design. The new colouring looks smoky and somewhat faded, so it appears to be even older than its antique parent. For a strikingly contrasting lone star, see the *Ode to Dale Evans Quilt* on page 39. It is slightly different in scale (it has 27 rows in the diamond blocks), but you could use it to inspire your colour plan for the format given here.

SIZE OF PATCHWORK
The finished *Lone Star Quilt* measures approximately 91in x 91in (231cm x 231cm).

SPECIAL FABRIC NOTES
This quilt is made entirely of Kaffe Fassett fabrics. Two of the fabrics, *Organic Stripe* and *Swiggle Stripe*, were designed specifically for quilts in this book and were based on antique fabrics on V&A quilts. Each of these stripes feature bands of several different print motifs, so that patches can be 'fussy' cut from specific areas. For this quilt, four different patch prints are taken from the *Organic Stripe* and three from the *Swiggle Stripe*, so if you are using your own fabrics for the quilt, be sure to use at least 12 different fabrics (instead of seven) for the diamond patches.

MATERIALS
Use 44–45in (112–114cm) wide cotton quilting fabrics
Diamond-patch fabrics: Seven KAFFE FASSETT fabrics as follows –

- 4½yd (4.2m) of *Swiggle Stripe* in Pink
- 2½yd (2.3m) of *Organic Stripe* in Brown
- 1yd (92cm) of *Damask* in Plum/Gold
- 1yd (92cm) of *Damask* in Sage
- ¾yd (70cm) of *Damask* in Smoky Blue
- ½yd (46cm) of *Peony* in Green
- ¼yd (25cm) of *Paperweight* in Sludge

Background fabric: 5yd (4.6m) of KAFFE FASSETT *Roman Glass* in Stone

REMAINING INGREDIENTS
Backing fabric: 8yd (7.4m) of desired fabric
Binding fabric: ¾yd (70cm) of KAFFE FASSETT *Broad Stripe* 06
Cotton batting: 98in x 98in (250cm x 250cm)
Quilting thread: Medium-toned neutral-coloured thread
Template: Use template ZZ (see page 139)

CUT PATCHES
Do not be tempted to use the strip-piecing method (sewing strips together, cutting at an angle and rejoining) for this quilt; if you do, the stripes will line up and look too regular.

DIAMOND PATCHES
The following list gives the number of template-ZZ diamond patches to cut for the entire quilt for each of the 17 rows in the eight lone-star blocks (for example, one diamond is cut for each of the eight lone-star blocks for row 1, for a total of eight diamonds). Note that the position of the fabric grain line alternates on the rows (see ZZ on page 139). Follow the correct grain line for each row so

that bias edges will be matched to straight-grain edges to stabilize the joined patches. The exception to this grain-line rule is for the rows where it says 'cut in several directions' – rows 2, 7, 9, 10, 11 and 17 – where the stripes should be cut facing at different angles with only *some* of the patches cut aligned with a template grain line. Keep the diamonds in marked piles for easy assembly of the blocks and so that the grain lines do not become mixed up.
Row 1 – 8 diamonds: Cut from Sludge *Paperweight*.
Row 2 – 16 diamonds: Cut these patches from the dark red ikat blotch section of Pink *Swiggle Stripe*, cutting in several directions so that the stripes look different (see photo of quilt on page 37) and ignoring the grain line on the template for most of the patches.

Row 3 – 24 diamonds: Cut from Plum/Gold *Damask*.

Row 4 – 32 diamonds: Cut from the seaweed section of Brown *Organic Stripe*.

Row 5 – 40 diamonds: Cut from Smoky Blue *Damask*.

Row 6 – 48 diamonds: Cut from Sage *Damask*.

Row 7 – 56 diamonds: Cut in several directions from the small stripe section of Brown *Organic Stripe*.

Row 8 – 64 diamonds: Cut from Green *Peony*.

Row 9 – 72 diamonds: Cut in several directions from the small stripe section of Pink *Swiggle Stripe*.

Row 10 – 64 diamonds: Cut in several directions from the dark red ikat blotch section of Pink *Swiggle Stripe*.

Row 11 – 56 diamonds: Cut in several directions from the large stripe section of Brown *Organic Stripe*.

Row 12 – 48 diamonds: Cut from Plum/Gold *Damask*.

Row 13 – 40 diamonds: Cut from the dots section of Brown *Organic Stripe*.

Row 14 – 32 diamonds: Cut from Sage *Damask*.

Row 15 – 24 diamonds: Cut from Smoky Blue *Damask*.

Row 16 – 16 diamonds: Cut from the seaweed section of Pink *Swiggle Stripe*.

Row 17 – 8 diamonds: Cut in different directions from the dark red ikat blotch section of Pink *Swiggle Stripe*.

BACKGROUND PATCHES

The dimensions for the background pieces given below are the ideal measurements. But because the diamond lone-star blocks are tricky to make an exact size, you may prefer to cut the background pieces a bit larger, sew them in place and then trim them once the quilt top is assembled.

4 large background corner squares: From Stone *Roman Glass*, cut four 26½in (67.3cm) squares.

4 large background edge triangles: From Stone *Roman Glass*, cut one 40in (101.6cm) square, then cut this square in quarters by cutting diagonally from corner to corner in both directions, to make a total of four quarter-square triangles.

MAKE LONE-STAR BLOCKS

Following the diagram for the row colours, arrange the diamond patches of each of the eight lone-star blocks. Match a bias edge to a straight-grain edge where possible. Using the seam allowance marked on the templates throughout, sew each of the blocks together in diagonal rows as shown, then join the rows. Press well.

ASSEMBLE TOP

Sew the eight lone-star blocks together, pressing the seams open and stopping each seam ¼in (6mm) from the outside edge of the star shape. Press the completed star very well.

FABRIC KEY

= **row 1** Sludge *Paperweight*

= **rows 2, 10, 17** Pink *Swiggle Stripe* (ikat blotch section)

= **rows 3, 12** Plum/Gold *Damask*

= **row 4** Brown *Organic Stripe* (seaweed section)

= **row 5, 15** Smoky Blue *Damask*

= **rows 6, 14** Sage *Damask*

= **row 7** Brown *Organic Stripe* (small stripe section)

= **row 8** Green *Peony*

= **row 9** Pink *Swiggle Stripe* (small stripe section)

= **row 11** Brown *Organic Stripe* (large stripe section)

= **row 13** Brown *Organic Stripe* (dots section)

= **row 16** Pink *Swiggle Stripe* (seaweed section)

Lone-star block

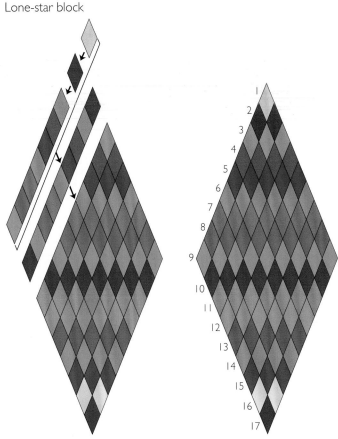

Inset the background corner squares and the background edge triangles. If necessary, trim the outside edge square, being careful not to cut off the tips of the star points.

FINISH QUILT

Press the quilt top. Layer the quilt top, batting and backing; and baste (see page 131).

Using medium-toned neutral-coloured thread, quilt in-the-ditch in the star and quilt long diagonal rows in the background areas. When the quilting is complete, trim the quilt edges. Then cut the binding fabric on the bias and attach (see pages 131 and 132).

Assembly – Lone-star Quilt

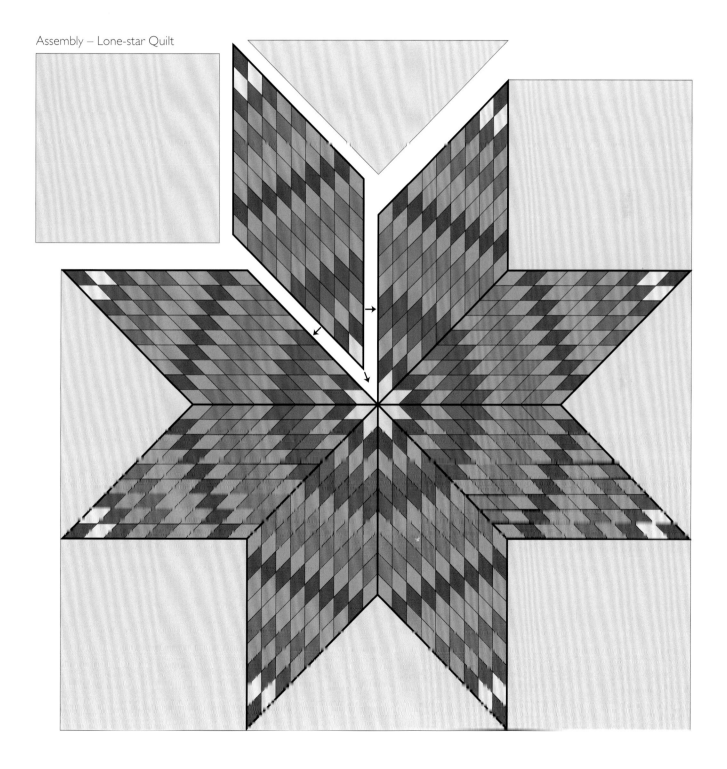

DOUBLE NINE-PATCH QUILTS

(pages 41–43)

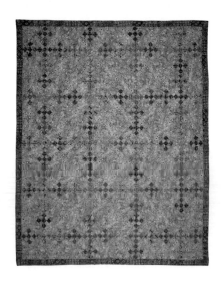

Although the colours may appear limited on these two *Double Nine-Patch Quilts*, they are definitely more colourful than the V&A inspiration which uses only cream and brown patches (see page 40). The *Spring Double Nine-Patch Quilt* has a light-toned lime background (see right and page 41). The tones on the *Winter Double Nine-Patch Quilt* are reversed, with the background darker than the medium-toned and medium-dark-toned jewel-coloured accents (see page 43).

SIZES OF PATCHWORKS

The finished *Spring Double Nine-patch Quilt [Winter Double Nine-patch Quilt]* measures approximately 71¼in x 88in (181cm x 223.5cm).

Note: The instructions for the *Spring Double Nine-patch Quilt* are given first and those for the *Winter Double Nine-patch Quilt* follow in brackets [ ]. (Only the fabrics differ.)

MATERIALS

Use 44–45in (112–114cm) wide cotton quilting fabrics

SPRING DOUBLE NINE-PATCH QUILT

KAFFE FASSETT fabrics as follows –

Main patch fabric: 5yd (4.6m) of *Paperweight* in Lime

Accent patch-fabrics: ¼yd (25cm) of each *Artichoke* in Pastel; *Diagonal Poppy* in Lavender and in Duck Egg; *Organic Stripe* in Blue; *Chrysanthemum* in Green; *Kashmir* in Blue and in Pink

Border fabric: ¾yd (70cm) of *Organic Stripe* in Pink

REMAINING INGREDIENTS

Backing fabric: 5¼yd (4.8m) of desired fabric
Binding fabric: ¾yd (70cm) of *Organic Stripe* in Pink

Cotton batting: 79in x 95in (201cm x 242cm)
Quilting thread: Light-coloured thread

WINTER DOUBLE NINE-PATCH QUILT

KAFFE FASSETT fabrics as follows –

Main patch fabric: 5yd (4.6m) of *Kimono* in Rust/Purple

Accent patch-fabrics: ¼yd (25cm) of each of *Shot Cotton* in the following 14 shades – Mustard, Persimmon, Scarlet, Navy, Cassis, Cobalt, Ginger, Mushroom, Jade, Chartreuse, Lettuce, Watermelon (tea-dye this colour to tint it slightly), Lavender and Grass

Border fabric: ¾yd (70cm) of *Wild Rose* in Crimson

REMAINING INGREDIENTS

Backing fabric: 5¼yd (4.8m) of desired fabric
Binding fabric: ¾yd (70cm) of *Exotic Stripe* No. 21
Cotton batting: 79in x 95in (201cm x 242cm)
Quilting thread: Medium-coloured thread

CUT PATCHES

FROM MAIN PATCH-FABRIC

4 corner triangles: Cut two 9⅜in (23.8cm) squares (aligning the patches with the straight grain of the fabric), then cut each square in half diagonally from corner to corner, to make a total of four half-square triangles.

14 edge triangles: Cut four 18¼in (46.4cm) squares, then cut each square diagonally from corner to corner in both directions, to make a total of 16 quarter-square triangles – only 14 of the squares are used, so use the leftover squares for smaller squares.

12 big squares: Cut 12 patches 12½in (31.8cm) square.

80 medium-size squares: Cut 80 patches 4½in (11.4cm) square.

400 small squares: Cut 400 patches that are a scant 1⅞in (4.7cm) square.

FROM ACCENT PATCH-FABRICS

500 small squares: Cut 100 sets of five patches that have been cut from the same fabric and are a scant 1⅞in (4.7cm) square. Be sure to cut the sets from all of the seven [14] accent patch-fabrics.

FROM BORDER FABRIC

4 border strips: Cut two side-border strips each 2½in x 84⅓in (6.4cm x 214.6cm) and a top- and bottom-border strip each 2½in x 71¾in (6.4cm x 182.3cm).

MAKE BLOCKS

Make the following blocks using a ¼in (6mm) seam allowance.

100 nine-patch blocks: Using five small-square patches in a single accent colour and four small-square patches in the main colour for each block, make 100 nine-patch blocks as shown in the diagram (see below).

20 double nine-patch blocks: Using five nine-patch blocks (with random accent colours) and four medium-size-square patches in the main colour for each block, make 20 double nine-patch blocks as shown in the diagram (see below).

ASSEMBLE TOP

Arrange the blocks and remaining patches, either on the floor or on a cotton-flannel design wall. First, place four double nine-patch blocks on point across the top, then place four more rows like this under the first row. Place the big squares cut from the main colour between the pieced blocks and position the edge and corner triangles along the sides and top and bottom. Make sure the accent colours are evenly distributed.

Once you have achieved the desired effect, sew together the pieces in diagonal rows, using a ¼in (6mm) seam allowance throughout and following the diagram (see below). Then sew together the diagonal rows.

Sew a long side-border strip to each side of the quilt. Sew the two remaining border strips to the top and bottom of the quilt.

FINISH QUILT

Press the quilt top. Layer the quilt top, batting and backing; and baste (see page 131).

Using a light-coloured [medium-coloured] thread, quilt a large blossom shape in the big plain squares and the edge and corner triangles. Quilt long straight lines through the points of all the small squares. The lines should run from top to bottom to create a striped appearance. Quilt meandering vines in the borders.

Trim the quilt edges. Then cut the binding fabric on the bias and attach (see pages 131 and 132).

FABRIC KEY

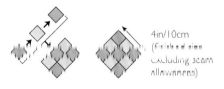

main fabric

border fabric

accent fabric

Nine-patch block

4in/10cm (finished size excluding seam allowances)

Double nine-patch block

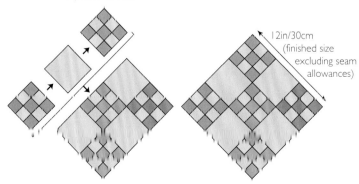

12in/30cm (finished size excluding seam allowances)

Assembly – Double Nine-patch Quilt

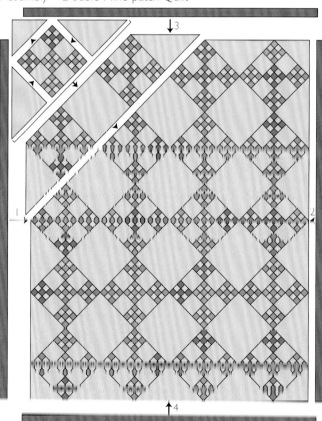

CLAMSHELL QUILT (page 47)

If you're looking for a challenging patchwork project, this may be the one for you. The entire quilt is made using the English paper-piecing technique. Hand piecing the clamshells together needs to be done with patience and accuracy. A much simplified interpretation of the original V&A quilt (see page 16), which uses squares instead of clamshell shapes, is shown on page 48 (see next page for instructions). For advanced quilt makers, here is a summary of how to make a version closer to the eighteenth-century original.

TO MAKE THE PATCHWORK
Only one template is used to make this quilt (see page 140). The finished size of the quilt is up to you. Keep adding diamond blocks until the quilt is the size you require or use fewer or more rows of clamshells for the diamond blocks.

FABRICS
Use your scraps and purchase extra fabrics as required. (We used KAFFE FASSETT fabrics. Outer border – *Lotus* in Red. Inner border – *Leaves* in Gold. Sashing and binding – *Shot Cotton* in Chartreuse. Clamshells – *Peony* in Maroon, in Red, in Green and in Blue; *Roman Glass* in Stone and in Jewel;

Bubbles in Ochre, in Sky Blue and in Plum; *Paperweight* in Sludge, in Pumpkin and in Cobalt; *Damask* in Sage, in Plum and in Jewel; *Blue-and-White Stripe 02*; *Diagonal Poppy* in Duck Egg and in Blue; *Paisley* in Raspberry; *Fruit Basket Toile* in Red; *Organic Stripe* in Blue, in Pink and in Brown; *Swiggle Stripe* in Blue, in Pink, in Green, in Antique and in Ochre.)

PAPER TEMPLATES
The English paper-piecing technique requires a paper template for each patch. Cut a single template with a seam allowance to trace the shapes onto the fabric, and cut paper templates without seam allowances for the piecing.

CUTTING PATCHES
Cut 49 clamshells for each diamond block. Cut as many patches from the same fabric as you need to form the symmetrical patterns in your blocks. For the four quarter-diamond corners, cut 16 clamshells each. For the half-diamonds blocks around the edges, cut 28 clamshells each.

PIECING
Lightly mark the two bottom seam lines on the right side of each clamshell patch so that the clamshells can be accurately overlapped. Pin a paper template to the wrong side of each patch, fold the long top curved edge to the wrong side and baste through the paper and fabric.

Once the top curves are basted in place, the clamshells are ready to be pieced together. To improve the accuracy of your piecing, pin the patches for each diamond block to a large piece of cardboard or a cork board, ensuring that they are aligned in straight rows and perfectly overlapped. Then baste the rows of clamshells together across the top of each row in the diamond, removing the holding pins from the cardboard as you proceed. Next, invisibly stitch the clamshell together along the folded-under curved tops.

Make as many diamond blocks and partial blocks as needed in this way. When finished, press the blocks.

(Do not trim the edges of the partial blocks until the blocks are joined by the sashing.) Remove the basting and paper backings on all the clamshells at the centre of each block, but leave the papers on the clamshells around the edges of the blocks to keep the edges stable while the sashing is added.

BIAS SASHING
For the bias sashing, cut the sashing fabric into 1¼in (3.2cm) strips and join on the bias for continuous strips. Fold the strip in half lengthways using a ⅛in (3mm) seam allowance. Finger press the resulting tube flat, with the seam in the centre of the wrong side, then press. (There is no need to turn the tube inside out as the seam is on the wrong side of the strip.)

Stitch the sashing strip in place between the blocks, taking tucks as necessary at the points of the curves.

FINISHING
Remove the remaining papers. Trim the outer edge of the quilt to straighten it and machine baste the trimmed edges. Cut and add the borders. Then layer the quilt top batting and backing in the usual way (see page 131). Quilt as desired, then add the binding.

SQUARE CLAMSHELL QUILT (pages 48 and 49)

This quilt is a simplified version of the *Clamshell Quilt* (see page 46 for the V&A inspiration and the opposite page for instructions). The English paper-piecing method used for the *Clamshell Quilt* is only for advanced quilt makers, so if you would like to make something with a similar look but with half the effort, try this easy *Square Clamshell Quilt*, which is made up of square patches on-point. The curve in the quilting stitch suggests the hand-pieced clamshell shape. Cut entirely from Kaffe Fassett fabrics, the colour scheme is a riot of pinks, magentas and reds with touches of green and gold.

SIZE OF PATCHWORK

The finished *Square Clamshell Quilt* measures approximately 67¼in x 93½in (171cm x 236cm).

MATERIALS

Use 44–45in (112–114cm) wide cotton quilting fabrics
Square-patch fabrics: 19 KAFFE FASSETT fabrics as follows –

◆ ¼yd (25cm) each of *Paperweight* in Sludge and in Pumpkin; *Paisley Stripe* in Red and in Bright; *Diagonal Poppy* in Lavender; *Leaves* in Gold, in Jade and in Periwinkle; *Pansy* in Gold; *Lotus* in Red and in Antique; *Zinnia* in Antique, in Lime and in Magenta; and *Roman Glass* in Gold

◆ ½yd (46cm) each of *Wild Rose* in Lavender, in Crimson and in Ochre

◆ 1yd (92cm) of *Swiggle Stripe* in Pink
Inner-border fabric: ¾yd (70cm) of KAFFE FASSETT *Kashmir* in Pink
Outer-border fabric: 1½yd (1.4m) of KAFFE FASSETT *Leaves* in Red (this is also used for small sashing squares)
Sashing fabric: 1yd (92cm) of KAFFE FASSETT *Organic Stripe* in Pink

REMAINING INGREDIENTS
Backing fabric: 5¼yd (4.8m) of desired fabric
Binding fabric: ¾yd (70cm) of KAFFE FASSETT *Paisley Stripe* in Red
Cotton batting: 75in x 101in (191cm x 257cm)
Quilting thread: Deep pink thread
Templates: Use templates U, V and VV (page139)

CUT PATCHES

Cut the borders and sashing pieces first, then cut the block patches.

4 inner-border strips: From Pink *Kashmir*, cut two strips 2½in x 78¾in (6.4cm x 200.4cm) and two strips 2½in x 56¾in (6.4cm x 144.2cm), piecing as necessary to make long enough strips.

4 outer-border strips: From Red *Leaves*, cut two strips 6in x 82⅞in (15.3cm x 210.5cm) and two strips 6in x 67¾in (15.3cm x 172.1cm), piecing as necessary to make long enough strips

24 sashing strips: From Pink *Organic Stripe*, cut 24 sashing strips each 1½in x 18in (3.8cm x 45.7cm), cutting so that all the patterns in the stripe show. (These strips are the same width as template W.)

7 sashing squares: Using template V, cut seven squares from Red *Leaves*.

10 sashing triangles: Using template VV, cut 10 triangles from Red *Leaves*.

Block squares: From the remaining fabrics, cut the squares for the clamshell blocks, using template U. Each block is made up of 49 squares. Start by cutting the squares for one clamshell block. First, 'fussy' cut the centre square, centring a motif in it (a flower or a distinctive feature of the chosen fabric). Then cut the 48 remaining squares from 12 different fabrics, cutting a set of four squares from each fabric. (Be sure to 'fussy' cut squares from the bold patterns.) Continue cutting template U squares in this way until there are enough for a total of 12 clamshell blocks. (Extra squares will be cut later for the partial blocks.)

ARRANGE CLAMSHELL BLOCKS

Arrange 12 clamshell blocks on the floor or on a cotton-flannel design wall. (Do not arrange them in the order they will be in the quilt yet, but just as 12 individual blocks.)

For each block, start with the 'fussy' cut centre square and arrange the patches outwards from the centre, positioning each of the sets of four identical-fabric patches in a symmetrical way around the centre.

This symmetrical arrangement can take many forms; study the photograph to see the variety of arrangements. Make sure that the patches are distinct and don't blend into each other.

MAKE CLAMSHELL BLOCKS

8 clamshell blocks: Choose the eight best blocks and sew the patches of these together as shown in the diagram (see right), using the seam allowance marked on the templates throughout.

6 half-clamshell blocks: Take three of the remaining clamshell blocks and separate each of them in half (see diagram of half-clamshell block). Cut and add extra matching squares along the centre where the block was separated in two (rather than cutting squares in half). Sew the patches of the half-clamshell blocks together, then trim the jagged edge straight, allowing ¼in (6mm) extra along this edge for a seam allowance. Stabilize the trimmed edges by machine-stitching a long basting stitch close to the cut edge.

4 quarter-clamshell blocks: Take the remaining block and separate this into quarters, cutting and adding matching patches where needed (see diagram of quarter-clamshell block). Sew the patches together, trim the edges and machine-baste the trimmed edges as for the half blocks.

ARRANGE TOP

Choose the two best full clamshell blocks and place these on-point in the centre (one on top of the other). Then arrange the remaining six full clamshell blocks around these as shown in the diagram (see next page). Move these blocks around until you are satisfied with the arrangement. Arrange the partial blocks around the edges.

ASSEMBLE TOP

Following the assembly diagram, sew the pieces of the patchwork together in diagonal rows — stitch the sashing squares and triangles to the sashing strips, and stitch the blocks together in diagonal rows with sashing strips between them. When all the diagonal rows of blocks and sashing strips are joined, sew the rows together.

Using a ¼in (6mm) seam allowance, sew one long inner-border strip to each side of the quilt, then the short inner-border strips to the top and bottom.

Sew on the outer-border strips in the same way.

FINISH QUILT

Press the quilt top. Layer the quilt top, batting and backing; and baste (see page 131).

Using a deep pink thread, quilt an arc inside each square to make it look somewhat like a clamshell. Stitch in-the-ditch between the sashing and the blocks. Quilt a meandering leaf pattern on the borders.

Trim the quilt edges. Then cut the binding fabric on the bias and attach (see pages 131 and 132).

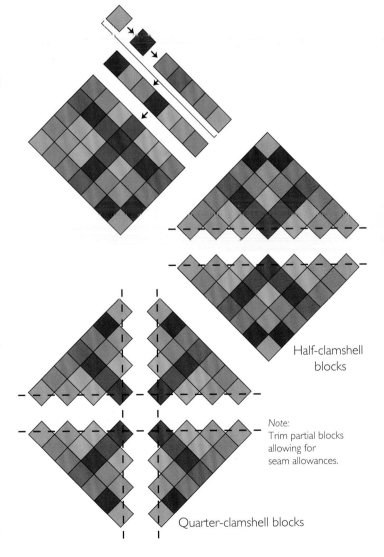

Clamshell block

Half-clamshell blocks

Note:
Trim partial blocks allowing for seam allowances.

Quarter-clamshell blocks

Assembly – Square Clamshell Quilt

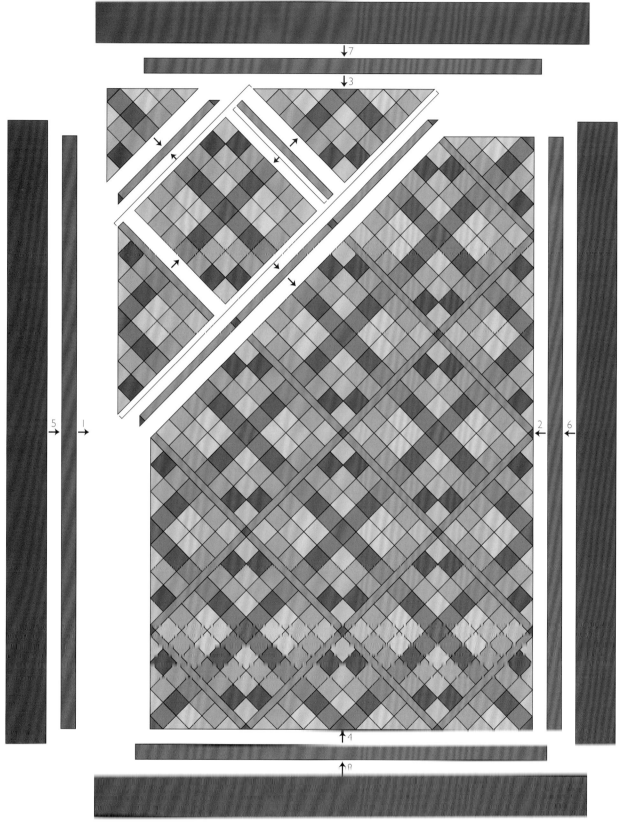

HOURGLASS QUILT (page 53)

Kaffe Fassett patchwork fabrics were used for this entire quilt, which is quite different in colour from the original V&A quilt that inspired it (see page 52). Although the colours are close in tone, they vary just enough to create the light/dark contrast that creates the traditional hourglass and pinwheel blocks. If you are making the quilt from a selection of your own scraps, be sure to keep in mind that you will need fabrics that can be grouped into two contrasting tone groups like this.

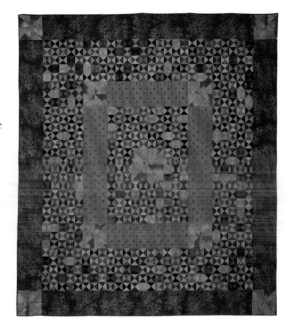

SIZE OF PATCHWORK

The finished *Hourglass Quilt* measures approximately 96in x 108in (244cm x 274.5cm).

MATERIALS

Use 44–45in (112–114cm) wide cotton quilting fabrics

Hourglass-block fabrics: ¼yd (25cm) each of assortment of KAFFE FASSETT fabrics (half of which are light-medium-toned to medium-toned and half of which are dark-medium-toned to dark-toned) as follows –

- ◆ *Shot Cotton* in 14 colours – Ginger, Tobacco, Pomegranate, Thunder, Pewter, Chartreuse, Mushroom, Lichen, Watermelon, Opal, Lavender, Grass, Prune and Pine
- ◆ *Roman Glass* in Gold, in Jewel and in Red
- ◆ *Fruit Basket Toile* in Gold and in Black
- ◆ *Peony* in Maroon
- ◆ *Artichoke* in Jewel
- ◆ *Dotty* in Plum
- ◆ *Exotic Check* No. 02
- ◆ *Narrow Stripe* No. 17
- ◆ *Alternative Stripe* No. 10

Pinwheel-block fabrics: ½yd (46cm) each of KAFFE FASSETT *Ikat Wash* in Red (a medium-toned fabric) and KAFFE FASSETT *Fruit Basket Toile* in Teal (a medium-dark-toned fabric)

BORDER FABRIC

Inner border: 1¼yd (1.2m) of KAFFE FASSETT *Ikat Dot* in Pumpkin

Outer border: 2½yd (2.3m) of KAFFE FASSETT *Fruit Basket Toile* in Red (leftover goes with hourglass-block fabrics)

REMAINING INGREDIENTS

Backing fabric: 9yd (8.3m) of desired fabric

Binding fabric: 1yd (92cm) of KAFFE FASSETT *Dotty* in Plum

Cotton batting: 103in x 115in (262cm x 292cm)

Quilting thread: Orange thread

Templates: Use templates R, S and T (page 140)

CUT PATCHES

Cut the borders first, then cut the patches.

Inner borders: From the inner-border fabric, cut two strips 9½in x 30½in (24.2cm x 77.5cm) and two strips 9½in x 42½in (24.2cm x 108cm).

Outer borders: To make long enough pieces for the outer border, first cut eight strips 9½in (24.2cm) wide from the outer-border fabric, cutting from selvedge to selvedge. Cut off the selvedges and sew the strips together end to end in a continuous strip. Then cut two strips 9½in x 78½in (24.2cm x 199.5cm) and two strips 9½in x 90½in (24.2cm x 230cm).

8 large pinwheel-triangles: For the large centre pinwheel, cut four template-R triangles from the medium-toned pinwheel fabric and four from the medium-dark-toned pinwheel fabric.

64 small pinwheel-triangles: For the eight small pinwheel blocks, cut 32 template-S triangles from the medium-toned pinwheel fabric and 32 template-S triangles for the medium-dark-toned pinwheel fabric.

584 hourglass squares (or 2,336 triangles): There are two ways to make the hourglass blocks. For the slower, more accurate method, cut 1,168 matching pairs of template-T triangles from the hourglass-block fabrics and the remaining border fabric. For the quicker method, cut 584 4¼in (10.8cm) squares from the hourglass-block fabrics and the remaining border fabric. (See diagrams and instructions below for two methods.)

MAKE PINWHEEL BLOCKS

For the large central pinwheel block, stitch together the eight large triangles as shown in the diagram (see below), using the seam allowance marked on the templates throughout. For each of the eight small pinwheel blocks, sew together four triangles from each of the two pinwheel fabrics as shown in the diagram.

MAKE HOURGLASS BLOCKS

Triangle-template method: To make the 584 hourglass blocks with the slower method, sew together two matching triangles from the darker-toned colour group and two matching triangles from the lighter-toned colour group as shown in the diagram (see below right), using the seam allowance marked on the templates throughout.

Quick method: To make the 584 hourglass blocks with the quicker method, select one square from the darker-toned colour group and one from the lighter-toned colour group. Place the squares right sides together with the lighter-toned fabric on top. Use a pencil to draw a diagonal line from corner to corner on the wrong side of the lighter-toned square. Sew a seam on each side of the diagonal line, each ¼in (6mm) from the line, then cut along the pencil line (see step 1, below). Press open each of the new two-tone squares, with the seam allowances pressed towards the darker-toned section. Next, place the squares right sides together, with the opposite colours facing each other. Draw another diagonal line from corner to corner so that it crosses the seam. Again, sew a seam on each side of the line, each ¼in (6mm) from the line, then cut along the pencil line (step 2). Press open each of the two finished hourglass blocks (step 3).

Make all 584 blocks in the same way.

ASSEMBLE TOP

Arrange the blocks, either on the floor or on a cotton-flannel design wall as shown in the assembly diagram (see page 102). Arrange the hourglass block rows so that the position of the darker-toned triangles alternate – a block with the darker-toned triangles in the north/south position next to one with the darker-toned triangles in the east/west position.

Once you have achieved the desired effect, join the hourglass panels by sewing the blocks together in rows and then joining the rows. For the centre, make two side panels

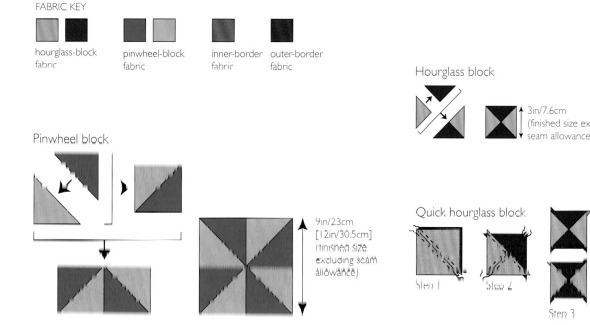

FABRIC KEY

hourglass-block fabric

pinwheel-block fabric

inner-border fabric

outer-border fabric

Pinwheel block

9in/23cm [12in/30.5cm] (finished size excluding seam allowance)

Hourglass block

3in/7.6cm (finished size excluding seam allowance)

Quick hourglass block

Step 1

Step 2

Step 3

three blocks by four blocks and top and bottom panels ten blocks by five blocks. For the outer hourglass border, make two side panels 20 blocks by five blocks and top and bottom panels 26 blocks by five blocks.

Starting at the centre, sew the two side hourglass panels to the large pinwheel, then sew on the top and bottom panels. Next, join the long inner-border strips to the sides of the centre. Sew a pinwheel block to each end of each of the short inner-border strips and join the strips to the top and bottom of the quilt centre.

Sew the two outer side hourglass panels to the quilt, then sew on the top and bottom panels. Join the long outer-border strips to the sides of the quilt. Sew a

pinwheel to each end of each of the two remaining outer-border strips and join the strips to the top and bottom.

FINISH QUILT

Press the quilt top. Layer the quilt top, batting and backing; and baste (see page 131).

Using an orange thread, stitch-in-the-ditch through and around each of the pinwheels and hourglasses. At each corner of the quilt top, quilt a sunrise shape in the centre of the pinwheel and quilt long 'rays' coming out of the sunrise.

Trim the quilt edges. Then cut the binding fabric on the bias and attach (see pages 131 and 132).

Assembly – Hourglass Quilt

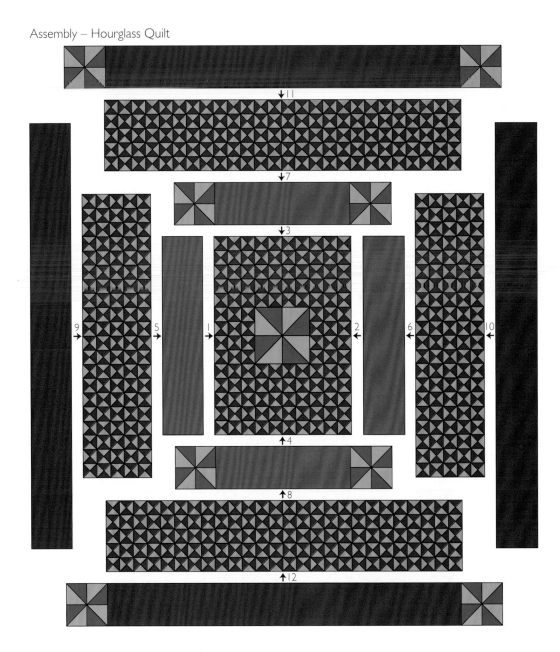

JOCKEY'S CAP BABY QUILT

(page 57)

This adaptation of a 1829 V&A patchwork (see page 56) takes its colour cues from the original, but is much smaller. As the quilt looks best when made up in as many different scraps as possible, a large collection of bits of antique reproduction fabrics would be the perfect ingredients.

This quilt is not for beginners. The centre appliqué and the block piecing involve lots of curves. It isn't terribly difficult to do, especially once you get the hang of it, but can be a little tricky for a first-time stitcher. For a simpler version, you can omit the appliqué at the centre and replace it with four more jockey cap blocks.

SIZE OF PATCHWORK
The finished *Jockey's Cap Baby Quilt* measures approximately 36in x 48in (91cm x 122cm).

MATERIALS
Use 44–45in (112–114cm) wide cotton quilting fabrics

APPLIQUÉ FABRICS
Background: 14in x 14in (36cm x 36cm) piece of medium-toned bluish pink solid-coloured fabric or very subtle print; and 4in x 14in (10cm x 36cm) piece of brown stripe, with the stripe running parallel to the short side
Vase: 6in x 8in (15cm x 20cm) of blue-and-white print
Flowers: Scraps of assortment of pastel stripes and dots in pink, blue and green on white
Leaves and stems: Scraps of leafy green solid-coloured fabrics or subtle prints

PATCHWORK BLOCK FABRICS
Fabric A: Scraps of at least 15 light-toned printed fabrics in denim blue, charcoal, chocolate, rust, dull rose, buff, ecru, cream, dusty lavender, grey, green-gold and indigo
Fabric B: Scraps of at least 15 dark-toned printed fabrics in the same colour family as fabric A

REMAINING INGREDIENTS
Backing fabric: 1½yd (1.3m) of desired fabric
Binding fabric: ½yd (46cm) of dark stripe (KAFFE FASSETT *Broad Stripe* No. 06 was used here)
Cotton batting: 43in x 55in (109cm x 140cm)
Quilting thread: Taupe thread
Templates: Use templates M and N and appliqué shapes (page 141), enlarging shapes as instructed

MAKE APPLIQUÉ TEMPLATES
Trace the appliqué shapes onto heavy, stiff paper (called card stock) and cut them out. Or, trace the appliqué onto freezer paper and cut out the individual shapes (see page 130).

CUT PATCHES
APPLIQUÉD CENTRE
Background: Cut a rectangle 12½in x 9½in (31.5cm x 24cm) from bluish pink fabric and a rectangle 12½in x 3½in (31.5cm x 9cm) from brown stripe, with the stripe running parallel to the short side.

Appliqué shapes: Using the templates, lightly trace each of the shapes onto the right side of the appliqué fabrics. (Alternatively, iron the freezer-paper shapes onto the fabrics.) Cut out each of the shapes, cutting ¼in (6mm) from the outer edge for the hem/seam allowance.

JOCKEY CAP BLOCKS
176 background shapes: Cut 88 template-M background shapes from fabric A and 88 from fabric B.
176 fan shapes: Cut 88 template N fan shapes from fabric A and 88 from fabric B.

SEW APPLIQUÉD CENTRE

Join the two appliqué background pieces together along two long edges using a ¼in (7.5mm) seam allowance. Press the seam open.

Prepare the appliqué pieces, stitching them together using your preferred appliqué method (see page 130).

With the right sides facing upwards, pin the prepared appliqué to the right side of the pieced background. Slip stitch the appliqué in place using fine thread and remove the basting. Then cut away the background fabric behind the appliqué to within about ¼in (6mm) of the slip stitching, so the background colour will not show through.

Press the finished appliquéd centre.

MAKE JOCKEY CAP BLOCKS

For each of the 44 blocks, select four background shapes – two in the same fabric A and two in the same fabric B; and four fan shapes – two in the same fabric A and two in the same fabric B. Stitch together each of the 44 blocks as shown in the diagram (see above right), using the seam allowance marked on the templates throughout. To make the piecing easier, clip the concave edge of the background shapes before pinning and stitching.

ASSEMBLE TOP

Arrange the blocks around the quilt centre, either on the floor or on a cotton-flannel design wall.

Once you have achieved the desired effect, sew together the six rows of six blocks (at top and bottom) and the four rows of two blocks (at sides of centre).

Next, join two of the short rows together for the left side section, and the two remaining short rows for the right side section. Join three of the long rows together for the top section, and the three remaining long rows for the bottom section.

Sew the two side sections to the appliquéd centre, then sew on the top and bottom sections.

FINISH QUILT

Press the quilt top. Layer the quilt top, batting and backing; and baste (see page 131).

Using a taupe thread, outline quilt the appliqué pieces and stitch veins in the leaves. Quilt small circles on the background around the appliqué.

Outline quilt a circle ¼in (6mm) inside the outer circular edge of each 'cap' and quilt circles in between each of the caps.

Trim the quilt edges. Then cut the binding fabric on the bias and attach (see pages 131 and 132).

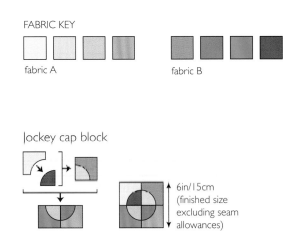

FABRIC KEY

fabric A   fabric B

Jockey cap block

6in/15cm (finished size excluding seam allowances)

Assembly – Jockey's Cap Baby Quilt

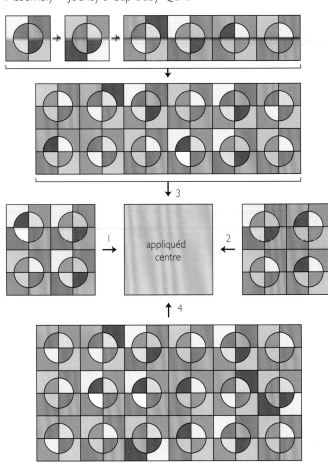

appliquéd centre

FOLK ART QUILT (pages 60 and 61)

The V&A inspiration quilt for this Kaffe Fassett design isn't really a quilt. It is an appliquéd coverlet with a backing and no quilting. It is a charming piece of folk art, featuring a huge variety of shapes of different sizes and themes.

This adaptation includes some of the original shapes and some new ones, and it is quick to make since the appliqué is applied with fusible web. It is likely that the original maker traced shadows cast by various objects to make her templates. This would be a wonderful quilt to tell a personal story. Just trace any object or project its shadow and trace that. Place the shapes in a pleasing manner, and voilà, a personalized folk art quilt!

SIZE OF PATCHWORK
The finished *Folk Art Quilt* measures approximately 94in x 94in (239cm x 239cm).

SPECIAL COLOUR AND FABRIC NOTE
A Kaffe Fassett fabric (in two colourways) was used for the background on this quilt. Alternatively, you can use another light taupe and/or light grey subtle, bicolour, patterned fabric. If you use two other fabrics, make sure they are very close in colour, as here. A solid fabric would not be as effective since so much background is visible.

For the border stripe, use a bold, wide stripe that is mostly deep blue. The one used here is a patterned stripe in mostly French blue, with a taupe accent.

See Materials, below, for the appliqué colour suggestions.

MATERIALS
Use 44–45in (112–114cm) wide cotton quilting fabrics
Appliqué fabrics: Assortment of scraps and ¼yd (26cm) lengths of at least 25 different medium-toned fabrics, including paisleys, stripes, plaids, spots, dots and bold, simple prints, all in bluish reds, pinks, magentas, dark plums, French blues, browns, ochres, lavenders and pine greens

Background fabric/s: A total of 6yd (5.5m) of one or two light-toned bicolour prints, in grey/white and/or taupe/white (see Special Note), or the two following KAFFE FASSETT fabrics
◆ 1½yd (1.4m) of *Peony* in Grey
◆ 4½yd (4.1m) of *Peony* in Taupe
Border fabric: 3yd (2.8m) of a medium-dark-toned, mostly in blue stripe (see Special Note), with the predominant blue stripe a minimum of 1½in (3.8cm) wide

REMAINING INGREDIENTS
Fusible web: 10–12 yd (9–11m) of lightweight fusible web (amount depends on width of web), for backing appliqué pieces and picket-fence edge of border
Backing fabric: 9yd (8.3m) of desired fabric
Binding fabric: ¾yd (70cm) of small-scale dark blue print
Cotton batting: 101in x 101in (257cm x 257cm)
Appliqué thread: Deep, bright magenta (or other bold colour)
Quilting thread: Off-white or pale grey thread
Templates: Use the 29 appliqué shapes (pages 142–146), enlarging as instructed

MAKE APPLIQUÉ TEMPLATES
Trace the 29 appliqué shapes onto heavy, stiff paper (called card stock) and cut them out.

CUTTING
Cut the pieces in the order given below.
25 large background squares: From the background fabric/s, cut twenty-five 15½in (39.4cm) squares.
4 border background strips: Cut the remaining

background fabric into strips 3in (7.6cm) wide and any length. Sew the lengths together end to end, then from this continuous strip cut four strips each 96in (244cm) long.
Appliqué shapes: Using the appliqué templates, trace the shapes onto fusible web. You will need one fusible web tracing for each appliqué shape on the quilt. Refer to the assembly diagram for how many of each shape to cut and for a guide to choosing fabrics. The appliqué pieces are used mostly in pairs of mirror images, so be sure to trace

the templates in reverse for the second piece of a pair. Roughly cut out the fusible web about ¼in (6mm) from the appliqué-shape outline. Fuse the fabric to the web following the manufacturer's directions. Using very sharp scissors to make clean cuts, cut out the appliqué pieces on the drawn line.

4 border strips: From the striped border fabric, cut strips 10in (25.4cm) wide and any length, with the stripe running widthways (see assembly diagram). Sew the lengths together end to end, pattern-matching the stripes carefully so the piecing is hidden. From this continuous strip, cut four strips each 96in (244cm) long – cut so that each length ends and begins with the same stripe (the easy way to do this is to fold the long length, matching up the stripes and trimming both ends). Next, cut strips of fusible web 2½in (6.4cm) wide. Fuse strips to the wrong side of one long edge of each of the four border strips. Butt the edges of web strips end to end along the border to make a continuous backing. Once the web is fused in place, the stripe is ready to be cut in a picket fence shape. Cut one stripe to a point and cut the next stripe straight across, about 1½in (4cm) below the point tip. When you have determined a shape that suits your stripe, make a little template to trace the shape along the edge of the border. On each border strip, trace the shape along the edge that has the fusible web, centring it on the border strip. Using very sharp scissors, cut out the picket fence shape along the fused edge. Then trim the straight outside edge of the border so that it is 9½in (24cm) wide from fence point to outside edge.

ASSEMBLE QUILT CENTRE

The top is very cleverly designed so that much of the appliqué can be applied to the background squares before they are assembled into a huge single piece (see assembly diagram right). This makes it simple to manipulate the fabric on the machine. It also makes this project very portable if you are hand-embroidering the appliqué edging.

Position the prepared appliqué shapes that do not cross over any seam line on the background squares – the positions do not have to be exact. Fuse these shapes in place on the background squares, following the manufacturer's instructions. Using a deep magenta thread, buttonhole or blanket stitch over the raw edge around each appliqué piece, machine- or hand-stitching.

When all of the appliqué pieces that are not on seam lines are sewn in place, start piecing the background squares together, using a ¼in (6mm) seam allowance throughout. Fuse on and edge the shapes that cross the seam lines as you progress. Press the completed quilt centre.

ASSEMBLE BORDER

Fuse the picket fence edge of the border strips to the border background strips, positioning the tips of the picket fence a little more than ¼in (6mm) from one raw edge of the background (this allows for the seam allowance). Using a deep magenta thread, buttonhole or blanket stitch over the raw edge all along the edge of the picket fence.

Pin the exact centre of one border strip to the exact centre of one side of the quilt centre, with right sides together. Carefully pin all along the length, making sure that the stripe ends up at exactly the same spot at each end. Make a mark ¼in (6mm) from each end of the quilt centre to indicate where to stop stitching. Sew on each border strip.

Mark the mitre on the four corners, using a 45-degree angle ruler as a guide. Sew the mitred seams along the marked lines and trim the seam allowance to ¼in (6mm).

FINISH QUILT

Press the quilt top. Layer the quilt top, batting and backing; and baste (see page 131).

Using an off-white or pale grey thread, 'echo' stitch around each object. The echos are repeated over and over around each object to form ripples. Quilt the border in straight lines so as not to break up the picket-fence effect.

Trim the quilt edges. Then cut the binding fabric on the bias and attach (see pages 131 and 132).

Assembly – Folk Art Quilt

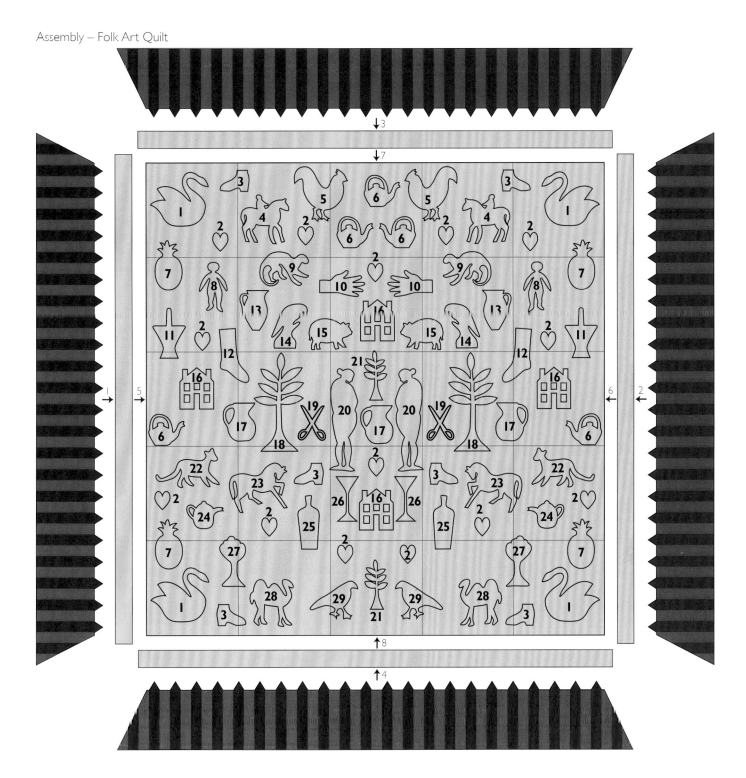

MARINER'S COMPASS QUILT (page 63)

Many of the quilts in this book are not close representations of the orginal antique V&A quilt. This one is an exception. It is very close in mood and scale to the original quilt (see page 62). Although the contemporary fabrics used are not period reproductions, they have the colour mood of the originals. The quilt format is quite true to the original quilt, so a quilter devoted to historical accuracy could have a wonderful time searching for 1820s reproduction fabrics to make this into a real period piece.

SIZE OF PATCHWORK
The finished *Mariner's Compass Quilt* measures approximately 99in x 99in (251.5cm x 251.5cm).

SPECIAL FABRIC NOTE
The more varied the collection of fabrics, the better your *Mariner's Compass Quilt* will be. If a specific fabric is needed in any section of the quilt, the amount is listed below under Materials. For the rest of the quilt, scraps or short lengths (¼–½yd/25–46cm) of a large variety of different fabrics is desirable. Paying attention to contrast and the tones of the colours (lightness and darkness) is essential, in order to make the block patterns work (see the diagram on page 111). Be sure to collect the fabric keeping this in mind.

The fabrics to collect are paisleys, dotty prints, stripes, calicos, medium-scale florals, monochromatic prints and plaids.

All of the fabrics specified in each part of the quilt would work fine in most other areas in the quilt. Mix and match freely, except where a specific fabric is designated.

MATERIALS
Use 44–45in (112–114cm) wide cotton quilting fabrics

QUILT CENTRE
Centre background: ½yd (46cm) of medium-toned gold calico
Circular compass-background: ½yd (46cm) of medium-dark-toned cocoa brown small-scale print
Four top compass arms: ¼yd (25cm) each of dark-toned cherry red monochromatic print and light-toned peach monochromatic print
Four north, south, east, west compass arms: ⅛yd

(25cm) each of dark-toned chocolate monochromatic print and light-toned ecru calico
Eight bottom compass arms: ¼yd (25cm) each of dark-toned plum monochromatic print and pale pink plaid or monochromatic print

BORDERS
For border no. 1: Assortment of 2–4 different light-toned dusty blues; and assortment of 2–4 different dark-toned cherry red small-scale prints and/or monochromatic prints
For border no. 2: Assortment of three different light- to medium-light-toned golds; and a total of ¼yd (25cm) of two different dark-toned polka dots in olive and/or brown
For border no. 3: A dark-toned cherry floral and a dark-toned brown floral; assortment of 2–4 dark-toned rusts and plums and assortment of light-toned prints in pink, in ecru and in aqua; assortment of 2–4 different dark-toned grey-plums, 2–4 different medium- and medium-light-toned taupes and beiges, and light-toned peach, dull light gold and dusty blue
For border no. 4: Assortment of dark-toned and medium-dark toned chocolates, plums, dusty blues and grey-plums; and assortment of light- and medium-light-toned ecrus, golds, roses, olives, peaches, taupes, dusty blues, sky blues, khakis and pumpkins
For border no. 5: ¼yd (25cm) of a dark-toned rusty red print; and fabrics as for border no. 4 border, plus light- and medium-light-toned lavenders
For border no. 6: 1½yd (1.4m) of a medium-dark-toned brown paisley and ½yd (46cm) of medium-dark-toned gold-brown paisley; plus 1½yd (1.4m) of a medium-toned sage-green print and ½yd (46cm) of a medium-toned lavender/brown stripe

REMAINING INGREDIENTS
Backing fabric: 9yd (8.3m) of desired fabric
Binding fabric: 3/4yd (70cm) of a red/plum/orange stripe (KAFFE FASSETT *Broad Stripe* No. 08 was used here)
Cotton batting: 106in x 106in (270cm x 270cm)

Quilting thread: Neutral-coloured thread
Templates: Use templates A, B, C and C reverse, D, E, F, G and G reverse, H, I, J, K, L and L reverse, and compass foundation piecing template (pages 146–150)

CUT PATCHES

QUILT CENTRE

Cut only the centre background at this stage; do not cut the other quilt-centre fabrics (for the central compass), because they are worked with a foundation paper and trimmed as they are used (see pages 129 and 130).

Centre background: From the background gold fabric, cut four 9⅛in (24.2cm) squares.

BORDERS

Border no. 1: Cut 112 template-A triangles from light-toned blue fabrics. Cut 28 template-B squares from dark-toned red fabrics.

Border no. 2: Cut 28 template-C and 28 template-C-reverse triangles from light- to medium-light-toned gold fabrics. Cut 28 template-D triangles from dark-toned olive and/or brown polka dot fabrics.

Border no. 3: Cut a total of 40 template-E squares from dark-toned cherry floral and a dark-toned brown floral. Cut 40 matching pairs of template-F triangles from dark-toned rusts and plums (for a total of 80 triangles) and 40 matching pairs of template-F-reverse triangles from light-toned pink, ecru and aqua (for a total of 80 triangles). Cut 40 each template-G and template-G-reverse parallelograms from mostly dark-toned grey-plums and some from other dark-toned fabrics (for a total of 80 parallelograms). Cut 40 each template-G and template-G-reverse parallelograms from mostly medium- and medium-light-toned taupes and beiges, and some from light-toned peach, dull light gold and dusty blue (for a total of 80 parallelograms).

Border no. 4: Each block in border no. 4 is made from four fabrics cut in matching pairs from the fabrics for border no. 4. Cut 28 matching pairs of template-H patches from the dark and medium-dark-toned fabrics and 28 matching pairs from the light- and medium-light-toned fabrics (for a total of 56 patches). Cut 28 matching pairs of template-I patches from the dark-and medium-dark-toned fabrics and 28 matching pairs from the light- and medium-light-toned fabrics (for a total of 56 patches).

Border no. 5: Cut 24 template-J triangles from a dark-toned rusty red print. From the remaining border no. 5 fabrics, cut 72 matching pairs of template-J triangles from light and medium-light tones (for a total of 144 triangles) and 60 matching pairs of template-J triangles from dark- and medium-dark tones.

Border no. 6: Cut 86 template-K triangles, two template-L triangles and two template-L-reverse templates from medium-dark-toned fabrics. Cut the same number of each triangle from the medium-toned fabrics. (It is quite difficult to piece the triangles for this border, so it is highly recommended that you mark the seam allowance on the wrong side of all the triangles.)

ASSEMBLE QUILT CENTRE

Using a ¼in (6mm) seam allowance, sew the four gold fabric squares together to make one 18½in (47cm) square for the centre quilt background.

Using the paper foundation piecing method (see pages 129 and 130), make four copies of the compass template on page 150. Then reverse the template and make four copies of this, for a total of eight paper copies of the foundation.

Sew the fabrics in the marked order to each of the eight foundation pieces. On the four compass pieces, use brown in area 1, pale pink in area 2, dark plum in area 3, brown in area 4, dark chocolate in area 5, and light peach in area 6. On the four reverse compass pieces, use brown in area 1, dark plum in area 2, pale pink in area 3, brown in area 4, ecru in area 5, and dark red in area 6. (Note that areas 1 and 4 are the background areas, so brown is used on both the compass and reverse compass pieces in these areas.

Trim the edges of the pieced wedges, leaving the marked ¼ (6mm) seam allowance around the outside. Sew the eight wedges together, alternating the compass and reverse compass pieces. (You can remove a little bit of paper ONLY from the pointed tip of each wedge to facilitate stitching, but leave the rest of the paper intact.) To make a neat, rounded circle, trim the seam allowance off the paper around the outside edge, then press the fabric seam allowance over the paper to the back.

Next, centre the compass circle on the gold background, using the background seam lines as a guide. Hand stitch the circle in place. Slit the background fabric behind the compass and cut it away, leaving a ¼in (6mm) seam allowance. Carefully, remove the paper.

ASSEMBLE BORDERS

Make the blocks for each of the borders using the seam allowance marked on the templates throughout and following the block assembly diagrams (see right).

Border no. 1: Make 28 blocks using one template-B square and four template-A triangles for each block. Then sew two borders of six blocks and two borders of eight blocks. Sew shorter borders to the top and bottom of the quilt centre and longer ones to the sides of the quilt centre.

Border no. 2: Make 28 blocks using one template-C triangle, one template-C reverse and one template-D triangle for each block. Then sew two borders of six blocks and two borders of eight blocks. Making sure that the dark-toned triangles point outwards, sew the shorter borders to the top and bottom of the quilt and longer ones to the sides.

Border no. 3: This border has a more complicated colour combination, so arrange the patches before stitching the blocks together. The side borders are each made up of four blocks and the top and bottom borders of six each. Arrange the borders either on the floor or on a cotton-flannel design wall.

Look at the photo of the quilt and notice where the darker and lighter patches are placed and where the matching pairs of patches are positioned. For example, notice that where one block meets the next, the small template-F triangles are matching pairs. Each block consists of two dark-toned template-E centre squares; four dark-toned and four light-toned template-F triangles; two darker-toned and two lighter-toned template-G parallelograms, two darker-toned and two lighter-toned template-G-reverse parallelograms.

Be sure to sprinkle in some unexpected bits of colour here and there in the small triangles and the parallelograms to enliven the border arrangements. Once you have achieved the desired effect for the four border strips, sew together the patches to make the 20 blocks. Then sew two borders of four blocks and two borders of six blocks. Sew the shorter borders to the sides of the quilt and the longer ones to the top and bottom.

Border no. 4: Make 28 jockey's cap blocks using one lighter-toned and one darker-toned matching pair of template-H patches, one lighter-toned and one darker-toned matching pair of template-I patches. Be sure to clip the inside curves on the template-H pieces to make stitching easier. Pin H and I together and stitch with H on top.

Then sew two borders of six blocks and two borders of eight blocks. Sew the shorter borders to the top and bottom of the quilt and the longer ones to the sides.

Border no. 5: Make a total of 36 blocks. Each block is made up of two different matching pairs of lighter-toned template-J triangles and two different matching pairs of darker-toned template-J triangles. Make sure that 12 of the blocks use two dark-toned rusty red triangles as the centre darker-toned matching pair (see the assembly diagram on next page).

Positioning the blocks with the rusty red triangles at regular intervals as shown on the assembly diagram, sew

Border no. 1 block

3in/7.5cm (finished size excluding seam allowances)

Border no. 2 block

4in/10cm (finished size excluding seam allowances)

Border no. 3 block
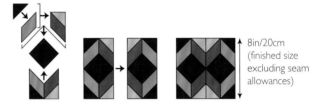
8in/20cm (finished size excluding seam allowances)

Border no. 4 block
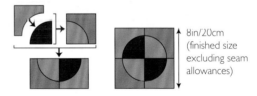
8in/20cm (finished size excluding seam allowances)

Border no. 5 block
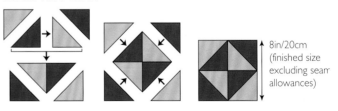
8in/20cm (finished size excluding seam allowances)

Border no. 6 block

8in/20cm (finished size excluding seam allowances)

two borders of eight blocks and two borders of 10 blocks. Sew the shorter borders to the sides of the quilt and the longer borders to the top and bottom.

Border no. 6

This border is not worked in blocks. Carefully pin the points when joining these triangles and follow the marked seam lines when stitching. Follow the assembly diagram when piecing the borders. The two side borders are made up of two darker-toned half triangles, and 20 lighter-toned and 19 darker-toned full triangles. The top and bottom borders are made up of two lighter-toned half triangles, and 24 darker-toned and 23 lighter-toned full triangles.

Making sure that the darker-toned triangles point inwards, sew the shorter borders to the sides of the quilt and the longer borders to the top and bottom.

FINISH QUILT

Press the quilt top. Layer the quilt top, batting and backing; and baste (see page 131).

Using a neutral-coloured thread, stitch in-the-ditch on the compass and echo quilt the wedges with two concentric lines in the brown wedges. Stitch small scallops throughout the gold background. On border no. 1 echo quilt inside the red diamonds and make oval leaf shapes in the blue triangles. On border no. 2 echo quilt three lines inside each triangle. On borders no. 3 and no. 4 stitch ⅛in (6mm) out from every seam. On border no. 5 echo quilt three lines inside each triangle.

Trim the quilt edges. Then cut the binding fabric on the bias and attach (see pages 131 and 132).

Assembly – Mariner's Compass Quilt

Compass centre

SUN AND MOON CUSHIONS (page 65)

These *Sun* and *Moon Cushions* are adaptations of patches from the King George III Reviewing the Volunteer Troops patchwork at the V&A (see page 64). The *Sun* is a true 'mariner's compass' that can be made quite easily using the paper foundation piecing method (see right and page 65). The *Moon* is a simple appliqué of concentric circles (see next page and page 65). Both have painted faces. If you are deft at embroidery, you could embroider the faces instead.

SIZE OF PATCHWORK
The finished circle of the *Sun Cushion* and the *Moon Cushion* measures approximately 16in (41cm) in diameter. The size of the background square is adjustable.

MATERIALS
Use 44–45in (112–114cm) wide cotton quilting fabrics

SUN CUSHION
Sun face: ¼yd (25cm) of solid pale dusty peach (KAFFE FASSETT *Shot Cotton* in Blush was used here)
Inner ring of short rays: ¼yd (25cm) each of a pink on white 'toile' fabric and a sage green on dull chartreuse print
Outer ring of long rays: ¼yd (25cm) each of a blue on white small-scale print, a rose on white small-scale print, a monochromatic pink print and a green on white small-scale print
Background and cushion backing: 1yd (92cm) of a small-scale print on a pale ecru ground, with mostly the ground showing

MOON CUSHION
Moon face: ¼yd (25cm) of a solid pale dusty peach (KAFFE FASSETT *Shot Cotton* in Blush was used here)
Concentric rings: ½yd (25cm) each of a chocolate brown calico and a chalk blue small-scale print; ¼yd (25cm) of a rose on white small-scale print
Background and cushion backing: 1yd (92cm) of a small-scale print on a pale ecru ground, with mostly the ground showing

REMAINING INGREDIENTS
Templates: Use two foundation piecing templates for the *Sun* (page 151) and concentric rings template for the *Moon* (page 150), enlarging as instructed
Fabric paints or pens: For drawing face
Thread: Sewing thread for stitching patches and sewing on cushion-cover back.
Cushion pad/pillow form: To fit cushion

MAKE TEMPLATES
SUN CUSHION
Make eight copies of the paper foundation piece for the outer ring of sun rays. Use the template for one-quarter of the inner ring to make a paper foundation piece of the full ring. Make a circle template 4in (10cm) in diameter for the face patch (this does not include the seam allowance).

MOON CUSHION
Using the moon template, make a template for the full circle with concentric rings. Trace the entire template onto

freezer paper. Cut in a straight line from the outer edge to the centre circle, then carefully cut out the centre circle, followed by each of the rings.

ASSEMBLE THE SUN
OUTER RING OF RAYS
Using the paper foundation piecing method (see pages 129 and 130), sew the fabrics in the marked order to each of the eight paper foundation pieces for the outer ring of rays. For area 1, use the pink monochromatic print; for area 2, use the green on white fabric; for areas 3 and 4, use

the pale ecru background fabric; for area 5, use the blue on white print; and for area 6, use the rose on white print.

Trim the edges of the eight pieced patches, leaving the marked ¼ (6mm) seam allowance. Sew these eight pieces together, leaving the paper in place. To make a neat, rounded outer edge, trim the seam allowance off the paper around the outside edge, press the fabric seam allowance over the paper to the back and baste in place.

INNER RING OF RAYS
Again using the paper foundation piecing method, sew the fabrics in one direction around the paper foundation piece, alternating the two colours. For the inner triangles, use the sage green and chartreuse print; for the outer triangles, use the pink on white toile print.

Trim the edges of the pieced patch, leaving the marked ¼ (6mm) seam allowance around the outside and the inside of the ring. Baste the outer seam allowance in place as for the outer ring of rays.

SUN FACE
Using the circle template for the face patch, lightly draw a circle on the right side of a piece of the face fabric, leaving excess fabric around the edge. Draw the face, then trim away the fabric ¼in (6mm) from the marked outline. Baste this circle to the paper template as for the rings.

Hand stitch the inner ring of rays to the outer ring and the face circle to the inner ring of rays. Then centre the finished sun patchwork on a 20in (51cm) square of the background fabric and hand stitch in place.

Slit the background fabric behind the sun patchwork and cut it away, leaving a ¼in (6mm) seam allowance. Carefully, remove the basting and the paper.

ASSEMBLE THE MOON
Press the largest ring of freezer paper onto the wrong side of the chocolate brown calico. Cut out the patch, cutting the fabric about ½in (12mm) from the paper. Along the outer edge only, press the seam allowance over the paper to the back and baste in place.

Prepare the three remaining rings in the same way, using the dull blue fabric for the next ring, the chocolate brown fabric for the next ring and the rose on white print for the smallest ring.

Press the centre circle of freezer paper onto the wrong side of the face fabric and cut out the patch as for the rings. Draw the face. Then baste the seam allowance to the wrong side as for the rings.

Starting with the two outer rings and adding the other rings one at a time to the ring underneath, hand stitch the rings to each other, ending with the face circle.

Slit the background fabric behind the moon patchwork and cut it away, leaving a ¼in (6mm) seam allowance. Carefully remove the basting and the paper

FINISH CUSHIONS
Trim the background fabric to a 17½in (44.5cm) square, or to the desired size including the seam allowance. Cut a cushion cover back the same size. With the right sides facing, sew the front and back together around three sides, leaving one side open. Insert the cushion pad/pillow form and sew the opening closed.

CHEQUERBOARD QUILT (page 67)

The pieced chequerboard blocks in this quilt have small patches by today's standards; when finished they measure 1½in (3.8cm) square. On the V&A original, however, some of the blocks have tiny ½in (6mm) squares (see page 66).

In order to echo the miniature antique squares, chequered prints were used here as faux tiny-square blocks. Dotty prints and plaids also give the feel of pieced chequerboards. Any dotty prints (especially traditional Provençal ones), as well as paisleys, stripes and solids are perfect for this contemporary interpretation.

If you really need to use up all those tiny scraps you have been saving, then replace the chequerboard fabrics with blocks of very small pieced squares. For each 6in (15cm) block with ¾in (2cm) finished squares, you'd need to cut and piece a total of 64 patches 1¼in (3.2cm) square. Still not as small as the patches on the original!

SIZE OF PATCHWORK
The finished *Chequerboard Quilt* measures approximately 109in x 109in (277cm x 277cm).

MATERIALS
Use 44–45in (112–114cm) wide cotton quilting fabrics
Edging-triangle fabric: 1½yd (1.4m) of KAFFE FASSETT *Pansy* in Brown (also used for some of the big square patches)
Centre medallion fabric: ½yd (46cm) of KAFFE FASSETT *Wild Rose* in Crimson
Centre medallion border fabric: ¼yd (25cm) of a medium-scale swirly stripe or paisley stripe in soft lavenders and purples
Centre medallion corners fabric: ¼yd (25cm) of KAFFE FASSETT *Diagonal Poppy* in Aubergine
Square patch fabrics: An assortment of KAFFE FASSETT fabrics and other fabrics as follows –
 ◆ ½yd (46cm) each of KAFFE FASSETT *Double Ikat Chequerboard* in Swede, in Magenta and in Gold
 ◆ ¼yd (25cm) each of KAFFE FASSETT *Pansy* in Cobalt; *Wild Rose* in Lavender; *Damask* in Sage; and *Shot Cotton* in Bittersweet, in Pomegranate, in Pine, in

Navy, in Mustard, in Charcoal, in Denim, in Stone Grey, in Slate and in Pewter
 ◆ ¼yd (25cm) of a soft medium-toned blue-green Provençal print or small-scale dotty print

More square patch fabrics: ¼–½yd (25–46cm) each of an assortment of KAFFE FASSETT fabrics and other fabrics for a total of at least 10yd (9.2m) as follows –
 ◆ KAFFE FASSETT *Narrow Check No. 03* in Red; *Broad Check No. 4* in Caramel; *Exotic Check No. 10* in Plum/Orange; *Damask* in Jewel and in Plum/Gold; *Pansy* in Gold; *Fruit Basket* in Red; and *Single Ikat Wash* in Banana and in Red
 ◆ Provençal prints or small-scale dotty prints in rusts, golds, deep tomato reds and corals
 ◆ Plaids, paisley prints and paisley stripes in rusts, plums, golds, browns and corals

REMAINING INGREDIENTS
Backing fabric: 9½yd (8.7m) of desired fabric
Binding fabric: 1yd (92cm) of KAFFE FASSETT *Broad Stripe No. 8*
Cotton batting: 116in x 116in (295cm x 295cm)
Quilting thread: Deep neutral-coloured thread
Templates: Use templates FF, GG and HH (see page 152)

CUT PATCHES
Be sure to cut the pieces in the order given here.

EDGING PATCHES
4 edging-triangle corners: From the edging-triangle fabric (Brown *Pansy*), cut two 5⅛in (13cm) squares, then

cut each square diagonally from corner to corner, to make a total of four half-square triangles.
48 edging-triangles: From the edging-triangle fabric (Brown *Pansy*), cut 12 patches each 9¾in (24.8cm) square, then cut them diagonally from corner to corner in both directions, to make a total of 48 quarter-square triangles.

CENTRE MEDALLION PATCHES

Centre medallion: From the centre medallion fabric (Crimson *Wild Rose*), cut the centre octagonal patch using template FF. (Be sure to enlarge template FF as instructed on page 152 to obtain the correct size for the centre medallion.)

8 centre medallion border patches: From the centre medallion border fabric (swirly stripe or paisley stripe), 'fussy' cut four template-GG and four template-HH patches.

4 centre medallion corner triangles: From the centre medallion corners fabric (Aubergine *Diagonal Poppy*), cut two 6⅞in (17.5cm) squares, then cut each square diagonally from corner to corner, to make a total of four half-square triangles.

CHEQUERBOARD PATCHES

Note that the format of the square patches in the *Chequerboard Quilt* is very symmetrical (see the large photograph of the quilt on page 67). Where there is an odd, off-beat colour or fabric, it occurs in exactly the same place in each quadrant (these fabrics in odd, off-beat fabrics include the *Ikat Chequerboards*, the Cobalt *Pansy*, and the green prints).

50 big square patches: First, cut 6½in (16.5cm) squares from seven specific fabrics (for using symmetrically) as follows – six Brown *Pansy*, four Cobalt *Pansy*, eight Swede *Double Ikat Chequerboard*, four Lavender *Wild Rose*, eight Magenta *Double Ikat Chequerboard*, eight total of Sage *Damask* and/or green Provençal print, and 12 Gold *Double Ikat Chequerboard*.

180 big square patches: Next, set aside all the solid-coloured *Shot Cotton* fabrics and divide all the other fabrics (not including those just cut) into two batches, one lighter batch and one darker batch. Cut a total of 80 patches 6½in (16.5cm) square from the lighter batch and 100 from the darker batch.

1216 small square patches: Use ALL the rest of the fabric (except the Brown *Pansy*) for the 76 chequerboard blocks. Each block requires eight 2in (5cm) light squares and eight 2in (5cm) dark squares. Cut enough for 76 blocks (a total of 608 light squares and 608 dark squares).

MAKE BLOCKS

Make a total of 76 chequerboard blocks using 16 small square patches for each of them. Make most of each block with two colours, but not just two fabrics. Make some of the blocks with mixed colours, but keeping the light/dark format.

Stitch together the 76 blocks as shown in the diagram (see right), using a ¼in (6mm) seam allowance.

MAKE QUILT CENTRE

Make the quilt centre first, using a ¼in (6mm) seam allowance throughout. First sew the template GG and template HH border pieces to the large octagonal medallion piece, then mitre the joins (sewing the mitred seams by hand is easier than by machine).

Lastly, sew the four triangles to the corners of the medallion.

ASSEMBLE TOP

Place the quilt centre either on the floor or on a cotton-flannel design wall and arrange the blocks and square patches around the centre.

First, position the Brown *Pansy* squares around the centre (in order to see where to place these patches, see the diagram on page 116 and the large photograph of the quilt on page 67). Fill in between these patches with gold fabric patches.

Then place the very specific fabrics (such as the *Ikat Chequerboards*) and fill in the rest of the area, paying attention to the placement of the lighter and darker square patches as you proceed.

Use a reducing glass or look through a camera during this process to keep the alternating darks and lights in the correct positions.

Position the pieced chequerboard blocks in two rows around the outside edge of the quilt, placing the different colourways at random. The row of plain squares between them is all lighter and mostly rose-plum-toned fabrics.

Once you have achieved the desired effect with the patches and blocks, sew together the pieces in diagonal rows, following the diagram (see page 116). Then sew together the diagonal rows.

Chequerboard block

6in/15cm (finished size, excluding seam allowances)

FINISH QUILT

Press the quilt top. Layer the quilt top, batting and backing; and baste (see page 131).

Using a deep neutral-coloured thread, stitch in-the-ditch in the pieced chequerboard blocks. Quilt the *Ikat Chequerboards* on the lines between the checks to make the grid more pronounced. Quilt a tiny chequerboard by stitching between the pansies in the inner *Pansy* blocks. Quilt meandering lines throughout the rest of the quilt.

Trim the quilt edges. Then cut the binding fabric on the bias and attach (see pages 131 and 132).

Assembly – Chequerboard Quilt

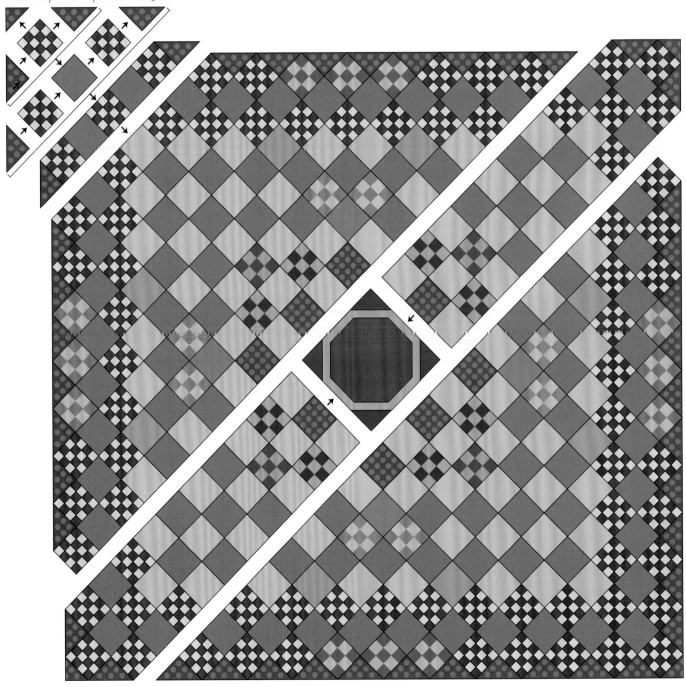

SAMPLER QUILT (pages 69–71)

The V&A original of the *Sampler Quilt* features a huge variety of printed fabrics, mostly in pink, blues, ecrus and browns (see page 68). This interpretation is very similar in feel to the old one. It uses the same basic structure, but the appliqué has been simplified and the tiny 4in (10cm) blocks in the antique quilt centre have been changed to just triangles. Traditional Dresden Plates take the place of the original sundial centre and the corner globes, keeping true to the lovely round shapes in the original.

SIZE OF PATCHWORK

The finished *Sampler Quilt* measures approximately 108in x 120in (274cm x 305cm).

SPECIAL FABRIC NOTE

All the fabrics used in this quilt are Kaffe Fassett fabrics. As the quilt is meant to be made with the feel of a scrap quilt, exact amounts are given only in the case of border fabrics and other main fabrics. The other amounts will depend on how each maker balances the colours.

Make this quilt your own by adding scraps from you own stash and by putting the block colours and fabrics together in combinations different from the ones shown here.

MATERIALS

Use 44–45in (112–114cm) wide cotton quilting fabrics
The following KAFFE FASSETT fabrics for specific areas of the quilt top –
Border no. 1 and borders 46, 47 and 48: 1½yd (1 4m) of *Diagonal Poppy* in Duck Egg
Border no. 2: 1¼yd (1.2m) of *Paisley Stripe* in Blue
Backgrounds for blocks ½ 43 and 43b: 1yd (92cm) of *Paperweight* in Pastel and 2½yd (2.3m) of *Paperweight* in Sludge
Half of each block 44: 1¼yd (1.2m) of *Shot Cotton* in Ecru
Triangle 45: ¾yd (75cm) of *Zinnia* in Magenta

Scrap fabric collection: Assortment of KAFFE FASSETT fabrics for all other patches as follows –
◆ 1yd (92cm) each of *Organic Stripe* in Pink and in Blue; *Swiggle Stripe* in Pink and in Ochre; *Fruit Basket* in Taupe
◆ ½yd (46cm) each of *Kashmir* in Pink and in Black; *Wild Rose* in Pastel: *Diagonal Poppy* in Blue; *Roman Glass* in Stone; *Shot Cotton* in Opal, in Tobacco and in Mushroom
◆ ¼yd (25cm) each of *Artichoke* in Pastel; *Pansy* in Grey and in Gold; *Kashmir* in Gold, in Blue, in Grey and in Aqua; *Fruit Basket* in Teal, in Gold and in Apricot; *Peony* in Ochre; *Zinnia* in Lime; *Paisley Stripe* in Mist; *Lotus* in Antique; *Blue-and-White Stripe No. 1*; *Shot Cotton* in Mustard, in Lichen, in Duck Egg, in Tangerine, in Watermelon, in Raspberry, in Ginger, in Putty, in Lilac, in Apple and in Lavender

REMAINING INGREDIENTS

Backing fabric: 10yd (9.2m) of desired fabric
Binding fabric: 1yd (92cm) of KAFFE FASSETT *Diagonal Poppy* in Blue
Cotton batting: 115in x 127in (292cm x 323cm)
Quilting thread: Neutral grey or neutral sage thread
Templates: Use templates for blocks 20, 38, 40, 41, 42 and 43 (pages 153–156); for the remaining patches, cut following the Cutting Guide and using templates on pages 157 and 158.

FOLLOW DIAGRAMS

Because this quilt is so complex, it is easier to follow diagrams than fully written instructions. One quarter of the symmetrical quilt is given in map form, with all the blocks and borders numbered for easy reference (see page 121). The miniature diagrams of the individual 6in (15cm) blocks (see page 119) are labeled with letters that indicate a specific triangle, square or rectangle listed in the Cutting Guide (see page 118) or a template given in the template chapter of the book. Templates for the bigger blocks are also given in the template chapter.

CUT PATCHES

Consult the photograph of the quilt when making your personal choice of patch colours, prints and tones; the block diagrams give an indication of how the light, dark and medium tones are arranged, but these are very simplified. Pay special attention to the clever use of stripes

GUIDE FOR CUTTING PATCHES
Use this guide to cut the triangle, square and rectangle patches for the 6in (15cm) blocks. The cutting sizes below include the seam allowances. The pieced blocks measure 6½in (16.5cm) before they are stitched together. (For templates AA–LL, see pages 157 and 158.)

hst = half-square triangle; first, cut a square that is aligned with the straight grain of the fabric, then cut the square in half diagonally from corner to corner (bisect) to make two triangles.

qst = quarter-square triangle; first, cut a square that is aligned with the straight grain of the fabric, then cut the square in half diagonally from corner to corner in both directions ('quadri'-sect) to make four triangles.

TRIANGLES
A **(hst)** – bisect a 2⅜in (6.1cm) square
B **(qst)** – 'quadri'-sect a 2¾in (7cm) square
C **(qst)** – 'quadri'-sect a 4¼in (10.8cm) square
D **(hst)** – bisect a 3⅞in (9.9cm) square
E **(hst)** – bisect a 1⅝in (4.2cm) square
F **(hst)** – bisect a 1⅞in (4.8cm) square
G **(hst)** – bisect a 3⅜in (8.6cm) square
H **(hst)** – bisect a 2⅞in (7.3cm) square
J **(qst)** – 'quadri'-sect a 3¼in (8.3cm) square

SQUARES
L – cut a 3½in (5cm) square
M – cut a 2in (5cm) square
N – cut a 2⅝in (6.7cm) square
O – cut a 1⅝in (4.2cm) square
Q – cut a 1¼in (3.2cm) square
R – cut a 1½in (3.8cm) square
S – cut a 1⅞in (4.8cm) square
T – cut a 2½in (6.4cm) square

RECTANGLES
U – cut a 2in x 3½in (5cm x 8.9cm) rectangle
Y – cut a 1½in x 2½in (3.8cm x 6.4cm) rectangle

within the blocks. 'Fussy' cut often. The original antique quilt featured many flowers and dots and stripes cut very carefully to achieve clever effects. When cutting each set of four blocks (for the four quarters of the symmetrical quilt design) be sure the colours are the same for all. It is best to sew the blocks as you cut the patches, but if you are not doing this, put the patches for each block, carefully labelled, in a small plastic bag or pin them together. There are MANY shapes that appear similar but measure slightly differently.

PIECES TO CUT FIRST
It is best to cut the biggest parts first; these are listed below. Next, read the section that follows about making the blocks and start your blocks by cutting the backgrounds for all the remaining big blocks. Then cut the patches for the smaller blocks, taking into account any special tips for the individual blocks.

Border no. 1 (inner border): From Duck Egg *Diagonal Poppy*, cut two side-border strips each 2½in x 110½in (6.4cm x 280.7cm), and a top- and bottom-border strip each 2½in x 102½in (6.4cm x 260.4cm).

Border no. 2 (outer border): From Blue *Paisley Stripe*, cut two side-border strips each 3½in x 114½in (8.9cm x 290.8cm), and a top- and bottom-border strip each 3½in x 108½in (8.9cm x 275.6cm).

Border 46 (diagonal edge of outside corners): From Duck Egg *Diagonal Poppy*, cut four strips each 2½in x 38in (6.4cm x 96.6cm) – the ends will be trimmed later.

Borders 47 (around quilt centre): From Duck Egg *Diagonal Poppy*, cut two strips each 3⅓ x 17⅓in (8.5cm x 44cm) and trim each end of these strips to a 45-degree angle.

Borders 48 (around quilt centre): From Duck Egg *Diagonal Poppy*, cut two strips each 2½ x 27¼in (6.4cm x 69.3cm) and trim each end of these strips to a 45-degree angle.

Backgrounds for block ½ 43: From Pastel *Paperweight*, cut two 12⅞in (32.7cm) squares and bisect diagonally from corner to corner to make four half-square triangles. From Sludge *Paperweight*, cut two more triangles in the same way.

Backgrounds for block 43b: From Sludge *Paperweight*, cut two 22⅛in (56.2cm) squares and bisect diagonally from corner to corner to make four half-square triangles.

Half of each block 44: From Ecru *Shot Cotton*, cut 312 H-triangles from 156 squares (see Cutting Guide). Cut the same amount of triangles from an assortment of the other PRINTED fabrics, avoiding solid colours.

Triangle 45: From Magenta *Zinnia*, 'fussy' cut 16 right-angled triangles that measure 6⅞in (17.5cm) along each short side, centring a flower in each patch.

MAKE BLOCKS
There are three basic types of piecing in this quilt: simple machine piecing, appliqué (see page 130) and paper foundation piecing which is then appliquéd to a background (see pages 129 and 130).

Sampler Quilt blocks

1 (F, H, S) 2 (A, B, G, M) 3 & 32 (D, S) 4 (A, B, G, M) 5 (AA, L) 6 & 28 (BB) 7 & 27 (T)

8 (A, C, N) 9 (F, J, S) 10 (F, J, Q, Y) 11 (H, J) 12 (CC, D, H, R) 13 (F, S, T) 14 (A, M)

15 (H, R) 16 (DD, EE) 17 (H, J, T) 18 (FF, GG, HH) 19 (F, II, S, Y) 20 21 (A, C, D, F, M)

22 (F, S, T, Y) 23 (C, D) 24 (F, J, S, T) 25 (M) 26 (H, T, Y) 29 (J) 30 (H)

31 (A, C, D, E, F, O) 33 (F, J, Q, Y) 34 (A, M, N, U) 35 (A, C) 36 (H, T) 37 (A) 38

39 (JJ, KK, LL) 40 41

42 — top half of block
(Dresden Flowers)

43 — top half of block
(Dresden Plate)

44

Note: Sizes shown are
finished sizes excluding
seam allowances.

= 1in/2.5cm

Read the tips below for the individual blocks. As you complete a block, do NOT trim it square. Because of the many tiny pieces and the different piecing techniques, the blocks may not come out to exactly the right size. It is preferable to ease blocks together; this ensures that points of patches are not cut off inadvertently. Fortunately, fabric is flexible and forgiving.

MAIN BLOCKS

The quilt is largely made up of 6in (15cm) blocks. (Note that this is the finished size, not including the seam allowances.)

Blocks 1–4: Make four of each of these blocks, following the Cutting Guide (see page 118) for the preparing the patches. Machine piece.

Block 5: As blocks 1–4, using the template on page 157 for AA.

Block 6: Machine piece, using template BB on page 157.

Blocks 7–11: As blocks 1–4.

Block 12: As blocks 1–4, using the template on page 157 for CC.

Blocks 13–15: As blocks 1–4.

Block 16: Machine piece, using templates DD, EE and EE reverse on page 157.

Block 17: As blocks 1–4.

Block 18: Machine piece, using templates FF, GG, HH and HH reverse on pages 157 and 158.

Block 19: As blocks 1–4, using the template on page 158 for II and II reverse.

Block 20: Make these four blocks using the appliqué and the paper foundation piecing methods. Use the template on page 153 to make a full block shape. Make a template of the inner circle and use this to lightly draw four circles on the right side of the chosen fabric. Cut out the fabric ¼in (6mm) from the drawn line. Next, make a template of the ring of wedges. Make four photocopies of this ring for the paper foundations for the four blocks. Make the ring of wedges, adding the fabric pieces in one direction around the paper ring – be sure to allow for a ¼in (6mm) seam allowance at the inside and outside of the ring (see pages 129 and 130 for how to work this technique). Fold under and baste the seam allowances on the rings and circles. Appliqué the ring to the background patch. Appliqué the centre circle to the ring. Cut away the background behind the appliqué and remove the paper and basting.

Blocks 21–26: As blocks 1–4.

Block 27: Make as for block 7, using different fabrics.

Block 28: Make as for block 6, using different fabrics.

Blocks 29–31: As blocks 1–4.

Block 32: Make as for block 3, using different fabrics.

Blocks 33–37: As blocks 1–4.

BIG BLOCKS

Make four each of all of the following blocks, except for blocks 40, 43a and ½ 43.

Block 38: Using the template on page 153, make with the same techniques as block 20.

Block 39: Machine piece, using templates JJ, KK, KK reverse, LL and LL reverse on page 158.

Block 40: Make only two of these blocks (see assembly diagram). Using the template on page 154, make the centre with the same techniques as block 20. Machine piece the corner triangles.

Block 41: Using the template on page 153, make the centre with the same techniques as block 20. Machine piece the border and corner triangles.

Block 42 (Dresden Flower): Using the template on page 155, make each of these blocks with the appliqué technique. Trace the petal shapes and the oval centre onto freezer paper. Press these templates onto the wrong side of the fabrics and cut out the shapes ¼in (6mm) from the edge of the paper. Baste the seam allowances to the wrong side around the oval centre, and around the petals (except for the seam allowance at the centre tips). Hand sew (whip stitch) the petals together where they touch. Machine piece the border strips and corners to the background piece. Then appliqué the circle of petals to the background, cut away the background behind the petals and remove the basting and paper. Sew the oval centre in place.

Block 43a (Dresden Plate): Make only one of this block for the centre of the quilt. Using the template on page 156, make the block with the same techniques as block 42, but note that the petal shapes are identical. Cut 16 petals for this block. Machine piece the border pieces and corners to the background piece.

Block 43b (Dresden Plate): Make as for 43a, but stitch to the triangle background.

Block ½ 43 (one half Dresden Plate): Make eight of these blocks with the same techniques as 43, but stitch to the triangle backgrounds. Use eight full petals for each block.

ASSEMBLE QUILT

Sew the patches together from the centre outwards, using a ¼in (6mm) seam allowance throughout. Note that when adding border 46, you should sew it first to the outer triangle (with the Dresden Plate on it). Pin the centre of the border to the centre of the large half-square corner triangle. Sew the border in place, press, then trim the strip ends so that they form a continuation of the short sides of the triangle. This section should measure 24⅞in (63.2cm) along the short sides.

FINISH QUILT

Press the quilt top. Layer the quilt top, batting and backing; and baste (see page 131).

Quilting can be very clever on this quilt top. Use a neutral grey or neutral sage thread and have fun. Each small block can be quilted in a different way. Emphasize the Dresden Plates and Fans with curved echo quilting and quilt the background behind them with a cross-hatch grid or clamshells. Quilt meandering lines in small areas. Quilt vines in the borders. It is not possible to go wrong.

Trim the quilt edges. Then cut the binding fabric on the bias and attach (see pages 131 and 132).

Assembly — Sampler Quilt

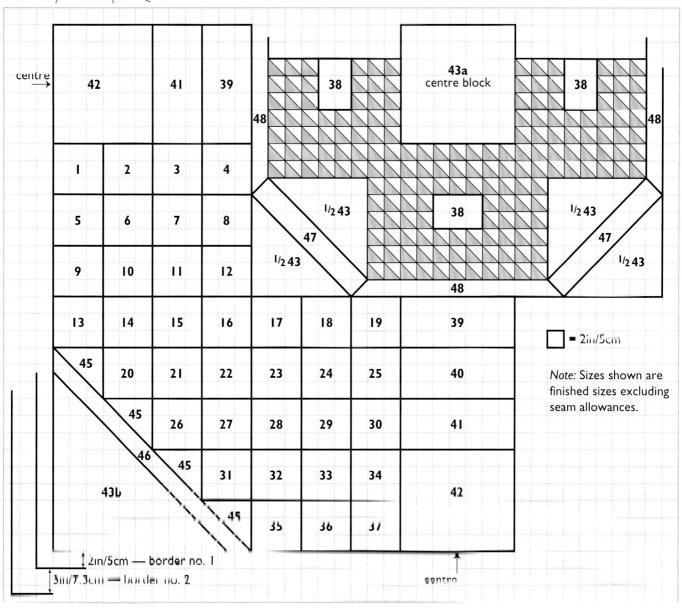

□ = 2in/5cm

Note: Sizes shown are finished sizes excluding seam allowances.

COMPLETE PATCHWORK
TECHNIQUES

The methods that follow are not meant to cover all the possible technical approaches to patchwork; they are merely the basics along with some very useful tips. Both hand piecing and machine piecing are covered. Those of you who want to carry your work with you may opt for the traditional hand piecing, but if you are keen on speedy results and have a sewing machine, you should try machine stitching your patchwork.

My advice is always the following – try not to get bogged down by the techniques. With practice the techniques will become second nature, and you will be able to enjoy concentrating on playing with colours within a patchwork geometry.

LEFT AND ABOVE The *Clamshell Quilt* (see pages 47 and 96).

PATCHWORK FABRICS

One hundred per cent lightweight cotton fabrics, specially produced for quilts, are the best materials to use for patchwork. Their advantages are that they have a firm weave, are easy to cut, crease and press, and are slow to fray. They also come in an astounding range of colours and prints, which means that the choice of palette is endless. The delicious textures and soft, subtle shades of some upholstery/furnishing fabrics do lend themselves to lovely patchworks, but they are not as easy to handle as lightweight cotton, and on some the cut edges fray very easily, so they are not recommended for beginners.

Liza and I are forever buying fabric for our stash. Just as an artist needs paints, the quilt maker needs a palette of fabrics. One thing to remember, is to look out for odd-coloured fabrics to add to your collection. Certain colours are easy to find – like cherry reds or navy blues – but if you come across an unusual greeny beige or chalky periwinkle, snatch up a quarter or a half a yard (25–46cm) to add to your palette. Stripes are also handy to collect for bias binding quilts – you'll need about ¾yd (70cm) for a bias binding for a bed-size quilt.

SCRAP FABRICS

In most of my patchwork designs, I like to use as many different fabrics as possible in order to make the colour composition interesting and lively. This makes the designs especially suited to the use of scrap fabrics, leftover pieces big enough for several patches.

If you are already a keen patchwork quilter, you will already have a collection of scraps that you are just waiting for the perfect opportunity to use up. Once you have chosen the quilt you want to make up, my advice would be to start assembling the colours you will need by going through your remnants. Add to this by purchasing small amounts of the missing colours, or even by finding suitable one hundred per cent cotton dresses, blouses or shirts in charity/thrift shops or jumble/rummage sales. Remember that polyester is more difficult to quilt than pure cotton and is crease resistant, which is not considered an asset for patchwork.

FABRIC COLOURS AND PATTERNS

Each set of instructions for the patchworks in this book gives either general fabric descriptions that are meant to be a guide to choosing fabrics or gives a detailed list of the Kaffe Fassett fabrics used (see page 159 for suppliers' addresses). Read the general fabric descriptions and study the photography carefully to decide on your fabric palette.

Many of the designs make use of monochromatic prints or tone-on-tone prints. These prints are composed of one colour in two or more tones – such as a mid and dark blue pattern on a light blue ground or a light blue pattern on a mid blue ground, etc. At a distance small-scale monochromatic prints can appear to be solid colours but have a much more interesting effect than solid-coloured fabrics. The patterns soften and add visual 'texture' to the patchwork geometry.

Many of the designs also use prints composed of three or more colours, such as those on large-scale floral and leaf prints. Even multi-coloured prints like these usually have a colour that predominates, so pay attention to this hue when selecting them. Alternatively, you can use only the areas of the print that suit your colour scheme, for example by framing the patches over the yellow flowers or only over the magenta flowers in a bold multi-coloured floral. (Cutting patches like this is called 'fussy' cutting.)

Always look at multi-coloured prints from a distance before buying them. For example, you may be looking for a fabric that is predominantly blue, you find one that looks blue with tiny yellow flowers, but when you stand away from it that perfect floral turns green!

Aside from prints, stripes, plaids and polka dots can also enliven a patchwork design. In some quilts, using all of these types of fabric pattern together definitely enhances the overall effect. Don't shy away from stripes because you think they may be hard to cut straight or match. There is no need to match stripes in patchwork, and there is no harm in the stripes being slightly off kilter – in fact, this can actually be done on purpose for an interesting effect, as on the *Lone Star Quilt* (see page 37 and page 91).

The only thing to remember when mixing fabrics is that they should all be about the same weight. If you stick to materials specially made for patchwork this will not be a problem because they are generally all the same lightweight, one hundred per cent cotton.

FABRIC QUANTITIES

Giving fabric amounts for a patchwork that uses a variety of prints is not an exact science, and quantities in instructions should only be considered an approximate guide. It is better to have too much fabric than too little and too many different prints than too few; excess can always be used up in future projects. Some of the instructions in this book give approximate amounts for the patches and others use so many different fabrics that a variety of scraps is recommended.

Keep in mind that running out of a particular fabric is not a tragedy – think of it as a design opportunity. Look for a fabric with a similar feel and use it to finish the job. One of the reasons antique quilts are so wonderful is the make-do philosophy of the makers. Those old quirky colour combinations born out of a this approach are charming, indeed.

If you are calculating exact amounts for borders, bindings or backings, remember that although specially made patchwork fabrics are usually 44in to 45in (about 112cm to 114cm) wide, the usable width is only about 42in to 43in (107cm to 109cm) due to shrinkage and the necessary removal of selvedges.

FABRIC PREPARATION

Always prewash cotton fabric before cutting it into patch shapes. This is a good test for colourfastness and also, if necessary, preshrinks the fabric. Be sure to wash darks and lights separately. Begin by soaking the fabric in hot soapy water for a few minutes, then look at the water to see if any colour has bled out. To be absolutely sure that the fabric is colourfast, press the wet fabric between white paper towels to check for bleeding.

Rinse the fabric well and when it is still damp, press it with a hot iron. After pressing, cut off the selvedges with a rotary cutter.

TOOLS AND EQUIPMENT

Very few tools are needed for patchwork. If you have a sewing workbox, you will probably already have the essentials – fabric scissors, pins, needles, a ruler, tape measure, ironing board and iron. This is all you need if you are making a simple 'squares' patchwork.

For other patch shapes you will need templates. These can be bought in various sizes or you can make your own. For this you will need graph paper, a ruler, a pencil, a pair of paper scissors or a craft knife, and for the template itself a piece of thin, stiff cardboard or specially made template plastic.

Probably the most useful patchwork tool to appear this century is the rotary cutter. With a rotary cutter, rotary ruler and rotary cutting board you can cut patches in straight, accurate lines in a fraction of the time it takes with

scissors. New gadgets for making patchwork quilts are always coming on the market and you should look around for anything you think will save you time and effort.

For machine piecing, of course, you will need a sewing machine. Quilting can also be done on a machine and requires a machine with a 'walking' or darning foot.

DESIGNING TOOLS

There are two invaluable tools that Liza and I use for designing: a design wall and a reducing glass. It is possible to arrange a full-size patchwork quilt on the floor, but when the floor space isn't available or if you need to be able to step back far enough to get a full view of the whole concoction, a design wall is just the thing.

Our design wall is large enough for working on a queen-size bed cover and is made with two 4ft by 8ft (about 122cm by 244cm) sheets of insulation board. Insulation board is a very light board about ¾in (2cm) thick; it has a foam core that is covered on one side with paper and on the other with foil. You could use any sturdy, lightweight board like this, but insulation board is especially handy as it can be cut with a craft knife. To make yourself a design wall, cover the two boards on one side with a good quality cotton flannel in a neutral colour such as dull light brown, taupe or medium grey. Then join the boards with three 'hinges' using a strong adhesive tape. Stick the hinges to the back of the boards so that you can fold the flannel sides together. The hinges will also allow you to bend the design wall slightly so it will stand by itself. If you need to put the wall away with a design in progress on it, just place paper over the arranged patches, fold the boards together and slide it under a bed.

A quilter's reducing glass looks like a magnifying glass but it makes things smaller. It helps you to see how a fabric

print or even a whole patchwork layout will look at a distance. Somehow, seeing the quilt layout reduced makes the errors in the design just pop out and become very obvious. Reducing glasses are widely available in shops that sell patchwork supplies. Looking through a camera is a good substitute.

PREPARING PATCHES

Once you have chosen all the fabrics for your quilt and prepared them (see above), you are ready to start cutting patches. Look at the patch shapes used for the quilt you are making. This will give you a good idea of how complicated or simple a patchwork will be to cut and piece.

Patches for designs made entirely of squares can be cut quickly and accurately with a rotary cutter, whereas triangle, parallelogram or trapezoid patch shapes will usually require templates for accurate cutting.

ROTARY CUTTING

Rotary cutting is especially useful for cutting accurate square patches and for cutting quilt border strips. The rotary mats and transparent acrylic rulers come in a range of sizes. Although it is handy to have a range of large and small mats and rulers, if you want to start out with just one mat and one ruler, choose an 18in by 24in (46cm by 61cm) mat and a 6in by 24in (15cm by 61cm) ruler. With a mat and ruler this size you can cut both border strips and patches with ease. The ruler will have measurement division markings on it as well as 90, 60 and 45 degree angles.

Before beginning to rotary cut, first press out any creases or fold marks on your fabric. Rotary-cut strips are usually cut across the fabric width from selvedge to selvedge, so you will need to straighten the raw end. Aligning the selvedges, fold the fabric in half lengthways and smooth it out. Keeping the selvedges together, fold the fabric in half again bringing the selvedges to the fold. On 44in (112cm) wide fabric there will now be an 11in (28cm) long edge to cut strips across.

Place the cutting board under the folded fabric and line up the selvedges with a line on the cutting board. Overlap the acrylic rotary ruler about ½in (12mm) over the raw edge of the fabric, using the lines on the cutting board to make sure that the ruler is perfectly perpendicular to the selvedges. Pressing down on the ruler and the cutter, roll the cutter away from you along the edge of the ruler. Open out the fabric to check the edge. Don't worry if the edge is not absolutely straight; a little wiggle won't show once the patches are stitched.

To cut a strip with a rotary cutter, first trim the raw edge of the folded fabric (see above), then align this trimmed edge with the markings on the ruler, keeping the ruler firmly in place and rolling the cutter away from you. Check intermittently to make sure that the raw edge is aligned with the correct position on the ruler.

To speed up alignment on the ruler, stick a piece of masking tape on the wrong side of the ruler along the measurement line that corresponds to the width you are cutting.

With practice you will easily be able to cut up to six layers of fabric with a large rotary cutter, thereby cutting several strips or patches at once. Be sure to change the cutter blade as soon as it shows the slightest hint of dulling.

Patches can be cut just as easily as strips. To cut square patches, first cut a strip the width of the square. Align one end of the strip with the correct markings on the ruler, then cut along the edge of the ruler, rolling the cutter away from you (see above).

MAKING TEMPLATES

You can cut patch shapes other than squares and strips with a rotary cutter – such as cutting diamonds from a strip, or half- or quarter-square triangles. For other shapes, however, it is best to use a template of the shape to draw onto the fabric or cut around. Standard-size templates are available in shops that sell patchwork fabrics and tools.

You can also make your own templates. The best material for a template is clear template plastic. Although it is easy to cut, it is very durable and will retain its shape despite being traced around time after time. Its other advantage it its transparency – you can see through it to frame fabric motifs. Thin, stiff cardboard can also be used if template plastic is not available.

To make a template, first trace the template shape provided with the quilt instructions, either directly onto template plastic or onto a piece of tracing paper and then onto thin cardboard. Use a ruler for drawing the straight lines and transfer the cutting line, the seam line and the grain line. Cut out the template.

Punch a hole in each corner at each pivot point on the seam line using a ⅛in (3mm) hole punch. This type of

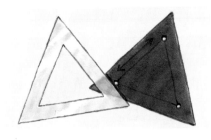

template is suitable for machine-pieced patches (see above right). For hand-pieced patches, you should ideally draw the seam line on the fabric and not the cutting line. The seam allowance can then be cut by eye around the patch. You may find that it adds to the accuracy of either machine or hand piecing to draw both the seam line and the cutting line on the fabric. For this you will need to make a window template from template plastic (see above left); this is basically just a frame as wide as the seam allowance.

Before going on to cut all your patches, make a block with test pieces to check the accuracy of your templates. This is especially important with blocks that require inset seams.

CUTTING TEMPLATE PATCHES

To cut template patches, place the template face down on the wrong side of the fabric, aligning the grain line arrow with the straight grain of the fabric (the crossways or the lengthways grain on the material).

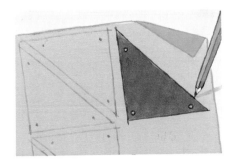

Press the template down firmly with one hand and draw around it with a sharp pencil in the other hand (see above). In order to waste as little fabric as possible, be sure to position the

patches as close together as possible or even touching.

You may notice when cutting patches from striped fabrics that although you are drawing around the patches on the straight grain, the outlines do not run exactly with the stripes. Do not worry about this. This will hardly be noticeable once the patches are pieced, and if it is, it just adds to the handmade quality of the patchwork. (On some patchworks you may want misaligned stripes on purpose.)

CUTTING REVERSE TEMPLATE PATCHES
A reverse template is the mirror image of a patch shape. If the instructions call for a template and a reverse template, the same template is used for both.

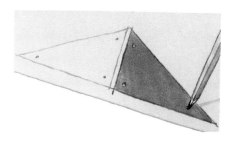

For the reverse of a template, lay the template face up on the wrong side of the fabric. Draw around the template in the usual way (see above).

BASIC HAND AND MACHINE PIECING

Patches can be joined together by hand or machine. Although machine stitching is much quicker, you might like the idea of being able to carry your patches around with you and work on them in every spare moment. Choose whichever method you find more enjoyable.

ARRANGING CUT PATCHES
Quilt instructions always give a layout for how to arrange the various patch shapes to form the overall geometrical design. It is, of course, possible to just pick your cut patches at random and stitch them together as you pull them out of the pile; but you will achieve a much better effect if you plan your colour arrangement before beginning to piece the patches together.

Lay the patches out on the floor or stick them to a large board covered with cotton flannel (see Tools and Equipment), then step back and study the effect. If you don't have access to such a large area, you can arrange individual blocks and, after the blocks have been stitched, arrange the completed blocks on the floor until you are satisfied with the layout.

Creating a stunning, vibrant colour composition is the most important part of the whole process of patchwork. You will notice that both the colour itself and its value will come into play in your arrangement. The value of a colour is its tone – which ranges from very light tones through to dark. Colours also have relative brightnesses, from dusty and dull to radiant and jewel-like. Dull colours appear greyer than others and tend to recede, while bright, intense colours stand out.

Make sure the colour arrangement is just right before starting to stitch the pieces together. Leave it for a few days and then come back to it and try another arrangement, or try replacing colours that do not seem to work together with new shades. Don't be afraid to position 'mistake' patches inside the arrangement to keep it lively and unpredictable. An unpredictable arrangement will always have more energy and life than one that follows a strict light/dark format.

If the quilt has no border or simply an uncomplicated strip border, it will be easy to change the size of the quilt at this point, but remember to cut any strip borders to the new size.

MACHINE PIECING
If you have a sewing machine, you'll be able to achieve quick results by machine piecing your patches together. Follow the instructions for the order in which to piece the individual patchwork blocks and then assemble the blocks together in rows.

The most important piecing tip for beginners is that you should use the same neutral-coloured thread to piece your entire patchwork. Taupe or light grey thread will work for most patchworks, except when the overall scheme is either very dark or very light. Be sure to purchase 100 per cent cotton thread.

Pin the patches together, right sides facing, and match the seam lines and corner points carefully. (You may find that you can stitch small squares together without pinning, so try both ways.) Then machine stitch, using the correct seam allowance (usually ¼in/6mm) and removing each pin before the needle reaches it.

Except for inset seams, machine stitched patchwork seams are sewn from raw edge to raw edge. (There is no need to work backstitches at the beginning and end of each patch seam, since the stitches will be secured by crossing seam lines as the pieces are joined together.)

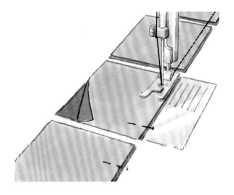

You can save both time and thread by chain piecing. This is done by feeding through the pinned together pieces one after another without lifting the presser foot. Let the machine stitch in the air a few times before it reaches the next pair of patches (see above).

PRESSING PATCH SEAMS

After each seam has been stitched, press the seams flat to embed the stitches. Then, if the patches have been chain pieced, cut them apart. Next, open out the patches and press the seam allowances to one side.

Continue joining the patches into blocks, then the blocks into rows as directed, pressing all the seam allowances in one row in the same direction. After all the blocks are joined into rows, join the rows together. Try to press the seam allowances in every other row in the opposite direction so that you don't have to stitch through two layers of seam allowances when joining the rows.

HAND PIECING BLOCKS

Hand stitching your patches together is time-consuming, but it does give a beautiful handmade finish to the patchwork.

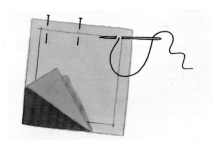

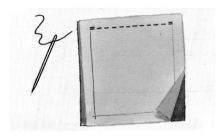

To hand piece two patches, pin them right sides together so that the penciled seam lines are facing outwards. Secure the thread end with a couple of backstitches (see above top). Then work short, even running stitches along the seam line, beginning and ending at the seam-line corners (see above).

When hand piecing, never stitch across the seam allowances. Press the seam allowances to one side as for machine-pieced seams, or press all seam allowances open.

STITCHING INSET SEAMS

You will find that most patches can be joined together with a straight seam line, but with some patchwork layouts a patch will need to be sewn into a corner formed by two other patches. This will require a seam line that turns a corner – called an inset seam. For example, on the *Lone Star Quilt* (see page 37), the big background pieces are attached with inset seams.

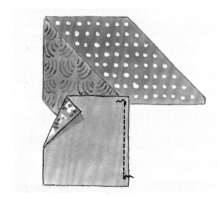

First, align the patches along one side of the angle and pin, matching up the corner points exactly. Machine stitch along the seam line of this edge up to the corner point and work a few backstitches to secure (see above).

Then pivot the set-in patch (see below) and align the adjacent side of it

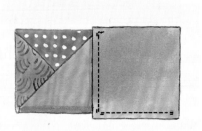

with the edge of the next patch so that the right sides of the two patches are facing each other. Carefully pin these two edges together (and baste if necessary – this may be helpful for a beginner). Beginning exactly at the corner point, work a few backstitches to secure the seam, then machine stitch along the seam line to the outer edge of the next patch and pin.

Trim away excess fabric from the seam allowance at the corner of the inset patch as necessary. (Remove any basting.) Press the new seams, easing the corner into the correct shape (see above).

PAPER FOUNDATION PIECING

In paper foundation piecing the patchwork block design is drawn on a piece of paper the exact size of the block. Each patch shape on the paper is numbered to indicate the sequence in which the patches should be stitched. During the stitching process, the patches are joined together under the paper foundation piece with the patch seams piercing the fabric layers and the paper.

This technique has many advantages. It requires little skill and is very accurate. It is also incredibly quick because there is no need for cutting patches with templates; all the fabric pieces can be cut in rough shapes and trimmed as they are stitched to the paper foundation.

Another advantage of paper foundation piecing is that it allows you to use patches that are not cut on the straight grain of the fabric. The paper provides the stability needed to keep the off-grain seams from stretching. Not having to pay attention to cutting exactly on the fabric grain line speeds up the piecing process considerably. It also enables you to design patchworks with stripes, plaids and prints set at random angles.

PREPARING PAPER FOUNDATIONS

You will need a paper foundation for each of the blocks being made with the technique. Either photocopy the diagram of the foundation piece or draw it on graph paper. If you are drawing the foundation-piece design, be as accurate as possible.

Always use a 'first generation' photocopy of the drawing as the master for the block design, since making a photocopy of a photocopy will distort the size and shape.

Cut out each paper foundation along the outer cutting line, which includes the seam allowance. If there are blocks of different sizes in the patchwork, check the master foundation pieces to make sure that they are all the correct size to fit together accurately.

CUTTING FABRIC PIECES

Before beginning to stitch the block, cut the fabric pieces for each of the numbered areas on the foundation piece. The size and shape of the fabric pieces need only be approximate. Try to allow for about a ⅛in (12mm) seam allowance, and if in doubt, cut the piece bigger rather than smaller.

The numbered side of the foundation paper is the wrong side of the block, so cut the fabric pieces with the wrong side facing up.

STITCHING THE BLOCKS

Once the fabric pieces are ready, insert a 90/14 machine needle. Then set the

sewing machine stitch length to a short stitch – about 18 to 20 stitches per inch (2.5cm). The large needle and short stitch will help to perforate the paper, making it easier to tear away later.

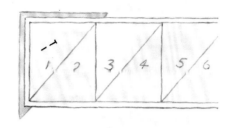

To start, take the roughly cut fabric piece for area no. 1 and pin it to the back of the foundation paper under area no. 1 of the block, with the wrong side of the fabric facing the unmarked side of the paper (see above). If in doubt as to the position of the patch, hold the paper up to the light to make sure that the fabric piece covers the area and extends a minimum of ¼in (6mm) beyond the stitching lines.

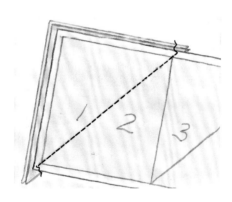

Next, place piece no. 2 on top of no. 1 (see above) with the right sides facing and the raw edges aligned along the seam-line edge. Holding the patches in place, machine stitch along the seam line between no. 1 and no. 2 with the marked side of the paper block facing upwards. Begin and end the stitching in the seam allowance so that it extends slightly beyond each end of the seam line as shown. The ends of the

stitching will be secured by future seams, so there is no need to start and end with backstitches.

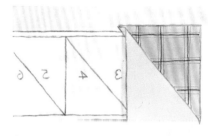

Trim the seam allowance of the seam just made to ¼in (6mm), using a small, sharp pair of scissors. Then open out piece no. 2 (see above), finger press the seam and press with a hot iron but no steam.

Continue adding pieces in this way, joining them in the sequence marked on the block.

After the last patch has been stitched in place on the foundation paper, trim away the excess fabric around the edge of the block with a rotary cutter and ruler, leaving the designated seam allowance around the outer edge of the finished block (see above).

Leave the paper foundation piece on the block until all the blocks have been stitched together, but tear out any paper corners that will make the seams too bulky. Note that the right side of the finished block is the reverse image of the marked side of the foundation

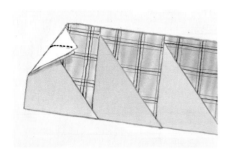

paper (see above). Once all the blocks are joined, tear away all of the paper.

APPLIQUÉ

A few quilts in this book use the technique of appliqué. Templates are provided for the shapes. Appliqué can be done in many different ways, and one of the quickest is needle-turn appliqué. To work needle-turn appliqué, first mark the right side of the appliqué fabric with a fine pencil or chalk line, tracing around each appliqué template. Then cut out the shape about ¼in (6mm) beyond the marked outline to allow for the hem/seam allowance. Pin the appliqué to the background. Start to turn under the edge with the needle and hold it in place just a little beyond where you will be sewing. Take a few fine slip stitches. Then continue in this way, turning under the edge and taking a few stitches. It may be necessary to clip inside curves and points, but don't do this until you are almost ready to sew that section.

The method that we prefer, however, is much more accurate than needle-turn appliqué, but is also much more time consuming. We use freezer paper to make each template. Freezer paper is widely available and can be found in most quilt shops, even though its original use was for wrapping meat for freezing. It comes on a roll like wax paper, and is a heavy white paper with a wax/plastic coating on one side. When the coated side is ironed onto fabric, it temporarily adheres to the fabric and doesn't leave a residue.

Prepare the appliqué by first tracing the whole image to be appliquéd onto the shiny side of the freezer paper. Number the pieces on the dull side, then cut them apart along the outlines. Trim each piece very slightly inside the traced line.

Iron each freezer-paper shape onto the WRONG side of its corresponding fabric. Cut out the fabric about ¼in (6mm) beyond the paper edge. Carefully turn the seam allowance to the back of the paper and baste in place. It may be necessary to clip at inside curves and points.

Next, sew each template-backed fabric to the adjacent ones using a fine thread. When the entire appliqué is sewn together, appliqué the complete piece to the backing fabric.

Once you have stitched your appliqué to the patchwork backing, cut away the backing behind the appliqué to within ¼in (6mm) of the seam. This keeps the fabric from becoming too bulky and keeps the colour of the backing from showing through. Carefully remove the basting threads and the freezer paper.

QUILTING AND FINISHING

After you have finished piecing your patchwork, press it carefully. It is now ready to be quilted if quilting is required. However, many items of patchwork, such as cushion covers, throws, curtains and table covers need only be backed.

QUILTING PATTERNS

Patchwork quilting is the stitching that joins together the three layers of the quilt sandwich – top, batting/wadding and backing. For patchworks that have a strong design story of their own, you may want to choose a quilting pattern that does not detract from the patchwork. In some instances you will find that stitch-in-the-ditch quilting is the perfect choice, since the quilting lines are stitched into the patch seam lines making the quilting stitches invisible on the right side of the quilt.

Outline quilting is another simple quilting pattern that will suit many patchwork designs. It is worked by stitching ¼in (6mm) from the patch seam lines.

You will need to mark more complicated quilting patterns on the right side of the pieced patchwork before the quilt layers are joined. The marking can be done with specially designed quilting markers. Using a quilting stencil is the easiest way to mark a complicated pattern on the fabric. These stencils are widely available in shops that sell patchwork and quilting materials.

If you are in doubt about which quilting pattern to chose, test the pattern on a spare pieced block. This will also be a good way to check whether your chosen quilting thread is a suitable colour. Quilting thread is a specially made cotton thread that is thicker and stronger than ordinary sewing thread. The thread colour should usually blend invisibly into the overall colour of the patchwork quilt when it is viewed from a distance.

PREPARING THE BACKING AND BATTING

Most large quilts need about 6–8yd (5.5–7.3m) of backing fabric. Liza and I are not fans of plain muslin on the quilt backs and prefer a print or stripe that looks good with the front. Liza tries to find half-price fabrics for backings.

To prepare the backing fabric, first cut the selvedges off, then seam the pieces together to form a backing at least 3in (7.5cm) bigger all around than the patchwork. It is best to join the pieces so that the seam lines run lengthways.

If the batting/wadding has been rolled, unroll it and let it rest before cutting it to about the same size as the backing. Batting comes in various thicknesses, but a pure cotton or mixed cotton and polyester batting that is fairly thin, will be a good choice for most quilts. Thicker batting is usually only suitable when the quilt layers are being tied together. A 100 per cent cotton batting will give your quilt the attractive, relatively flat appearance of an antique quilt.

BASTING THE QUILT LAYERS

Lay out the backing wrong side up and smooth it out. Place the batting on top of the backing, then lay the pieced patchwork right side up on top of the batting and smooth it out.

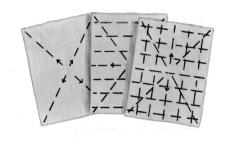

Beginning at the centre, baste two diagonal lines from corner to corner through the layers (see above left). Make stitches about 3in (7.5cm) long and try not to lift the layers too much as you stitch. Then, again always beginning at the centre and working outwards, baste horizontal and vertical lines across the layers (see above centre and right). The basting lines should be about 4in (10cm) apart.

HAND QUILTING

Hand quilting is best done with the quilt layers mounted in a quilting frame or hoop. Thread a short quilting needle (an 8 to 11 'between') with an 18in (46cm) length of special cotton quilting thread and knot the end. With the quilt top facing upwards and beginning at the centre of the basted quilt layers, insert the needle through the top about ½in (12mm) from the starting point and into the batting, then bring it out at the starting point. Pull the thread to pop the knot into the batting.

Loading about three or four stitches on to the needle and working with one hand under the quilt to help the needle back up again, make short, even running stitches. Pull the thread through and continue along the quilting line in this way.

It is more important to make even stitches on both sides of the quilt than to make small ones. When the thread is about to run out, make a small backstitch, then pierce this backstitch to anchor it and run the thread end through into the batting.

MACHINE QUILTING

For machine quilting, use a walking foot for straight lines and a darning foot for curved lines. Use regular sewing thread and choose a colour that blends with the overall colour of the patchwork for the top thread and one that matches the backing for the bobbin thread. Begin and end the quilting lines with very short stitches to secure, leaving long ends to thread into the batting later. Follow the machine manual for tips on using the walking or darning feet.

TYING QUILTS

If you don't have the time needed for allover quilting, you can tie together the basted layers of your quilt. For simple tying, cut a 7in (18cm) length of yarn and thread the needle.

Beginning the tying at the centre of the quilt, make a small stitch through all three layers (see below left). Tie the two ends of the yarn into a double knot (see below right) and trim. If you are making bows, use a longer length of thread.

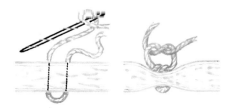

When tying quilts in this way, be sure to use a sharp needle with a large eye. Wool yarn, thick embroidery thread or narrow ribbon are all suitable for the tying.

You will find that tying works best on batting that has a high loft, because thin cotton battings usually require quite close quilting lines.

BINDING QUILT EDGES

Once the quilt has been quilted or tied together, remove the basting threads. Then baste around the quilt just under ¼in (about 5mm) from the edge of the patchwork. Trim the outer edge of the quilt, cutting away the excess batting and backing right up to the edge of the patchwork and, if necessary, straightening the edge of the patchwork in the process.

Cut 2in (5cm) wide binding strips either on the straight grain or on the bias. (Striped fabrics look especially effective when cut on the bias to form diagonal stripes around the edge of the patchwork.) Join these biding strips end-to-end with diagonal seams until the strip is long enough to fit around the edge.

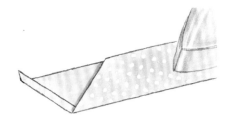

Cut the beginning end of the binding strip at a 45-degree angle, turn ¼in (6mm) to the wrong side along this cut end, and press. Then fold the strip in half lengthways with the wrong sides together and press (see above).

Place the doubled binding on the right side of the quilt, with the longer side of the left-hand end facing the quilt and the raw edges aligned. Stitch from the second folded edge on the binding ¼in (6mm) from the edge, up to ¼in

(6mm) from the first corner (see above). Make a few backstitches and cut the thread ends.

Continue stitching the binding in place all around the edge in this way, tucking the end inside the beginning of the binding (see above).

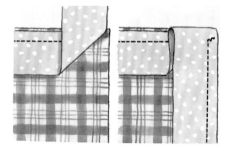

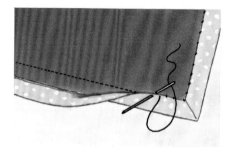

Fold the binding up, making a 45-degree angle (see above left). Keeping the diagonal fold in place, fold the binding back down and align the edge with the next side of the quilt. Beginning at the point where the last stitching ended, stitch down the next side (see above right).

Turn the folded edge of the binding to the back. Hand stitch in place, folding a mitre at each corner (see above).

LEFT The *Hourglass Quilt* (see page 53 and pages 100–102).

PROJECT TEMPLATES

The templates, appliqué shapes and paper foundation piece shapes for the patchworks are given on pages 134–158. Most of the templates are all shown actual size, and those that are shown reduced are accompanied by instructions.

The seam lines on the templates, appliqué shapes and paper foundation pieces are indicated by solid lines and the cutting lines by dotted lines. For a few of the shapes, you will have to add seam allowances yourself after tracing the shapes.

ABOVE A detail from the *Sampler Quilt* (see page 69 and pages 117–121).

LEAFY SNOWBALL QUILT

The instructions for the *Leafy Snowball Quilt* are on pages 82–83. The templates needed to make the quilt are shown here actual size. Template Q, on the right, is used for the corners of the blocks and includes the seam allowance, although it is not marked on the template. Templates Q and P are also used for the *Wedding Snowball Quilt* (see pages 84–86).

Q

SNOWBALL
PATCHWORKS

draw pencil line
on wrong side
of fabric

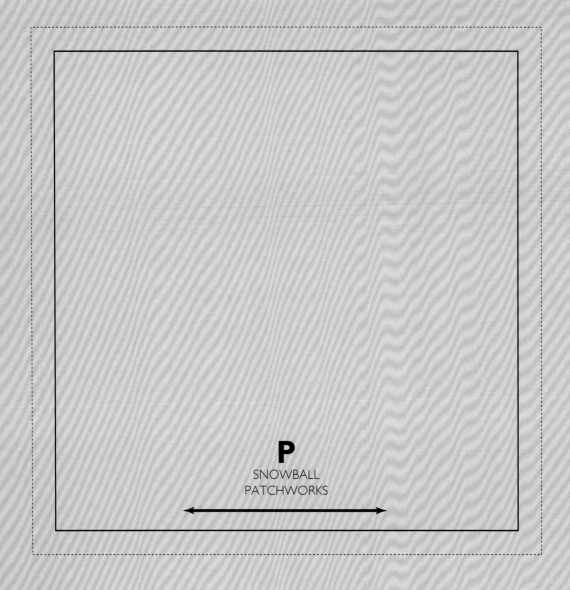

P

SNOWBALL
PATCHWORKS

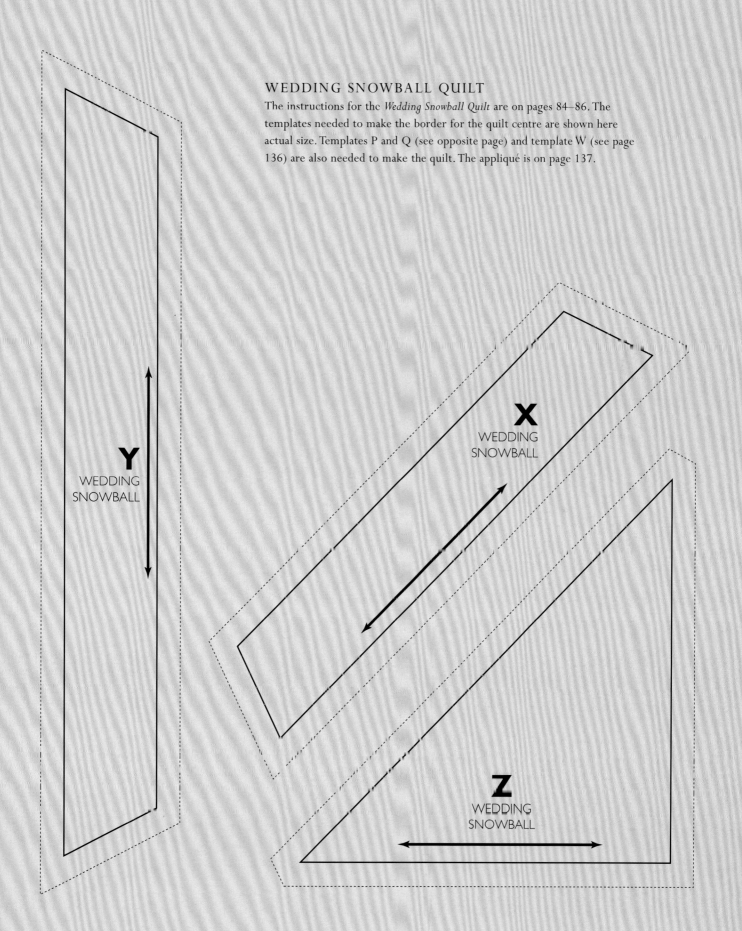

WEDDING SNOWBALL QUILT

The instructions for the *Wedding Snowball Quilt* are on pages 84–86. The templates needed to make the border for the quilt centre are shown here actual size. Templates P and Q (see opposite page) and template W (see page 136) are also needed to make the quilt. The appliqué is on page 137.

Y
WEDDING
SNOWBALL

X
WEDDING
SNOWBALL

Z
WEDDING
SNOWBALL

WEDDING SNOWBALL CENTRE

Template W is shown here actual size. It is one quarter of the background for the quilt centre. Copy this template four times to make the full template. The other templates needed for the *Wedding Snowball Quilt* are shown on pages 134 and 135.

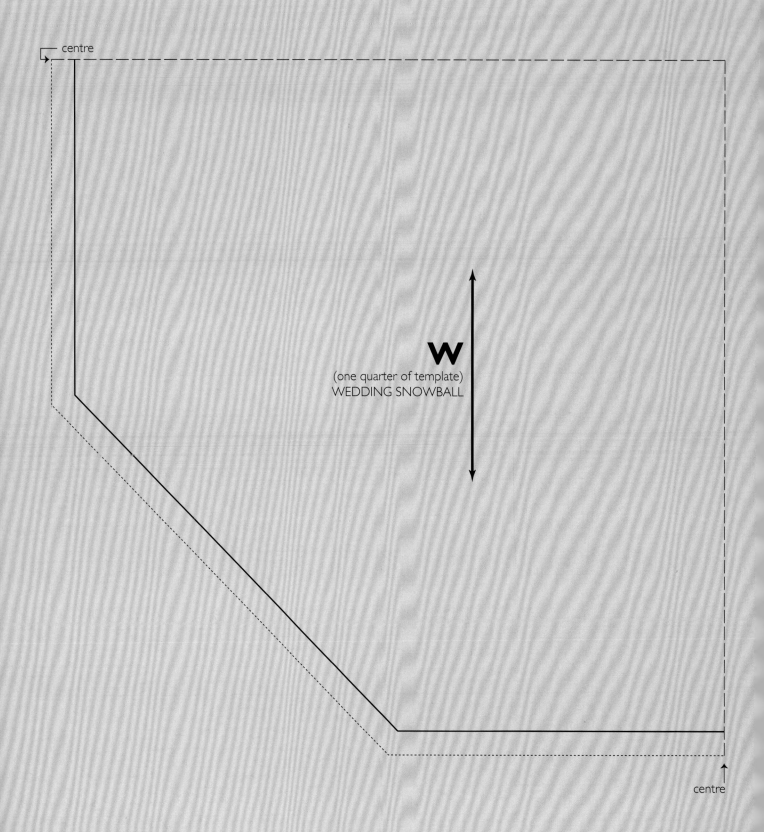

centre

W

(one quarter of template)
WEDDING SNOWBALL

centre

FABRIC KEY
A = light blue
B = white
C = apple green
D = blue-green
E = pinkish off-white
F = lilac
G = soft pink
H = deep gold
I = medium rose
J = pinkish lavender
K = pink and blue stripe
L = medium soft yellow
M = orange-yellow
N = pink, periwinkle and white stripe
O = red-orange
P = red and plum print

WEDDING SNOWBALL APPLIQUÉ

The appliqué bouquet for the centre of the quilt is shown here at 50 per cent of its actual size; enlarge 200 per cent for the correct size. The bouquet shapes are appliquéd to the centre background (template W on the opposite page). Follow the fabric key for the fabric colours.

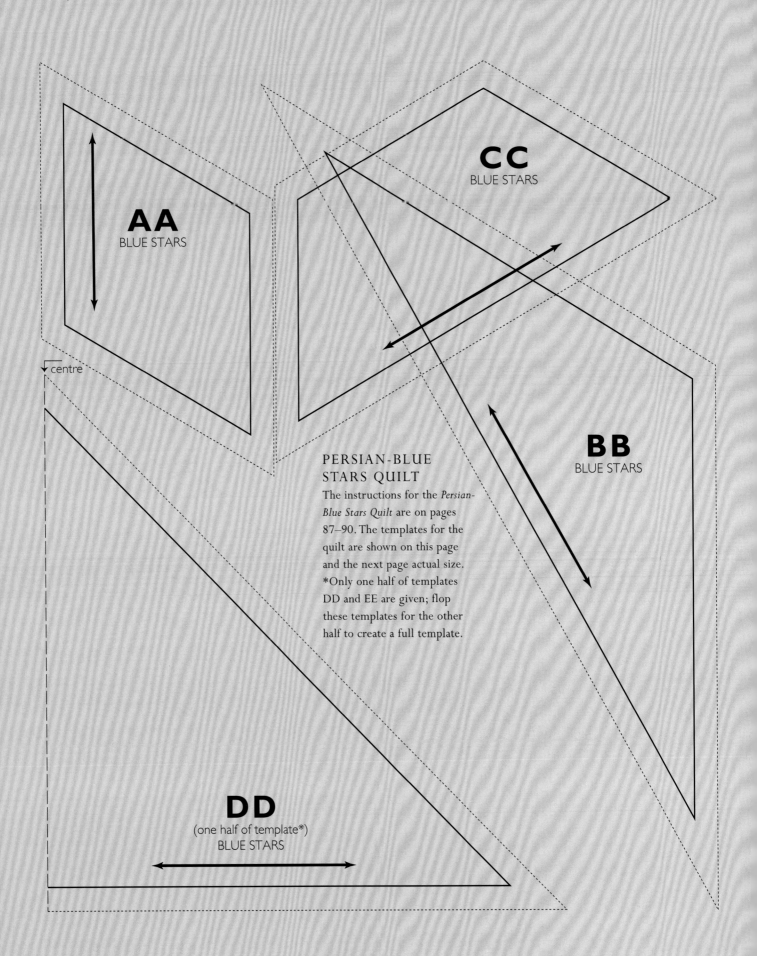

AA
BLUE STARS

CC
BLUE STARS

BB
BLUE STARS

centre

PERSIAN-BLUE
STARS QUILT
The instructions for the *Persian-Blue Stars Quilt* are on pages 87–90. The templates for the quilt are shown on this page and the next page actual size.
*Only one half of templates DD and EE are given; flop these templates for the other half to create a full template.

DD
(one half of template*)
BLUE STARS

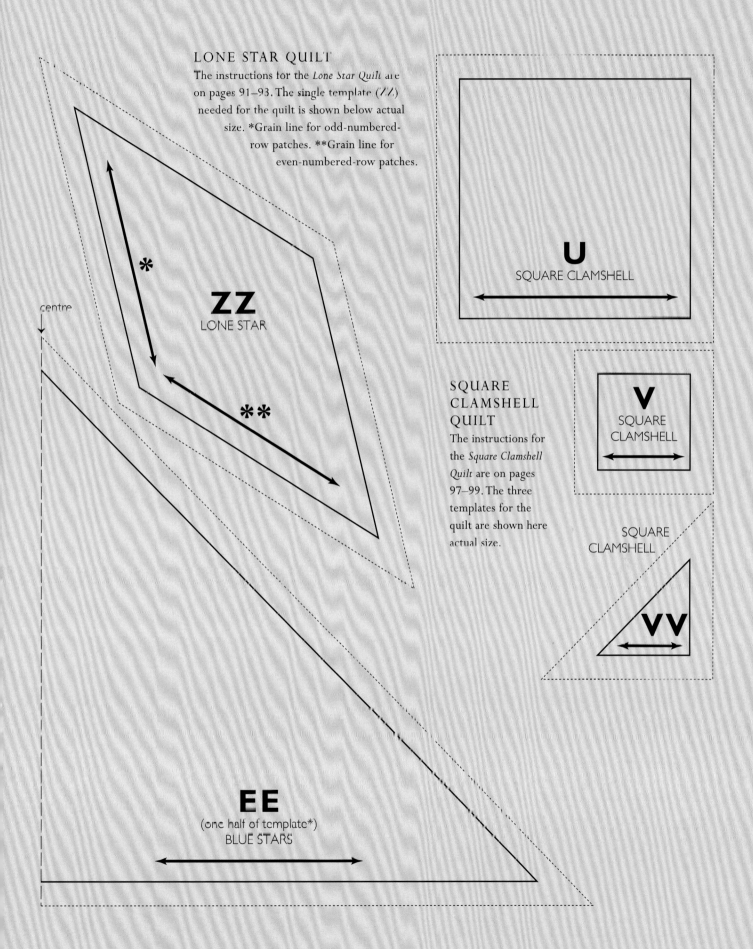

LONE STAR QUILT
The instructions for the *Lone Star Quilt* are on pages 91–93. The single template (*ZZ*) needed for the quilt is shown below actual size. *Grain line for odd-numbered-row patches. **Grain line for even-numbered-row patches.

*

ZZ
LONE STAR

**

centre

EE
(one half of template*)
BLUE STARS

U
SQUARE CLAMSHELL

SQUARE CLAMSHELL QUILT
The instructions for the *Square Clamshell Quilt* are on pages 97–99. The three templates for the quilt are shown here actual size.

V
SQUARE CLAMSHELL

SQUARE CLAMSHELL

VV

HOURGLASS QUILT

The instructions for the
Hourglass Quilt are on pages
100–102. The three templates
for the quilt are shown here
actual size.

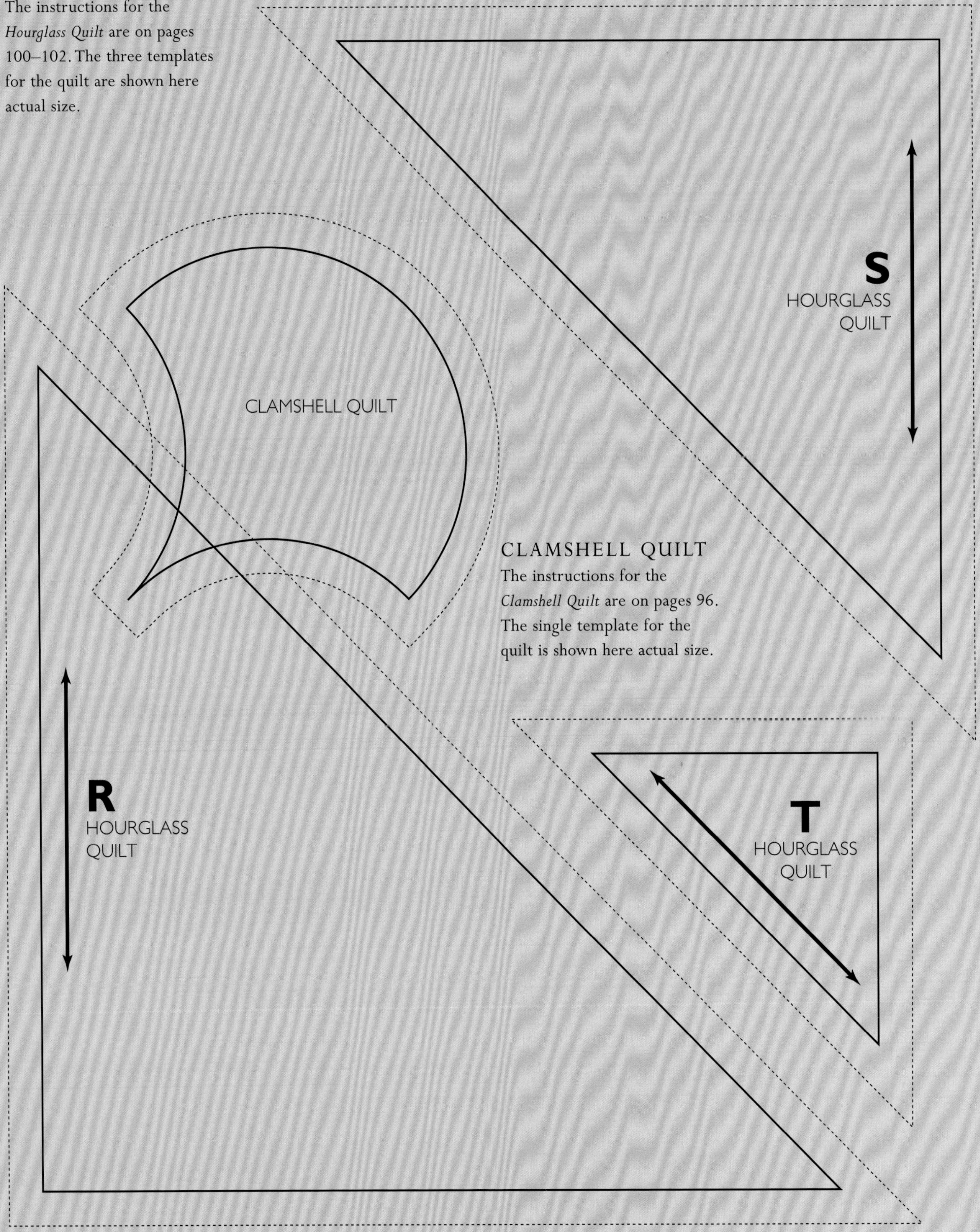

S
HOURGLASS
QUILT

CLAMSHELL QUILT

CLAMSHELL QUILT

The instructions for the
Clamshell Quilt are on pages 96.
The single template for the
quilt is shown here actual size.

R
HOURGLASS
QUILT

T
HOURGLASS
QUILT

JOCKEY'S CAP BABY QUILT

The instructions for the *Jockey's Cap Baby Quilt* are on pages 103–104.
The appliqué vase of flowers at the centre of the quilt is shown below
at 50 per cent of its actual size; enlarge 200 per cent for the correct
size. Templates M and N are shown actual size.

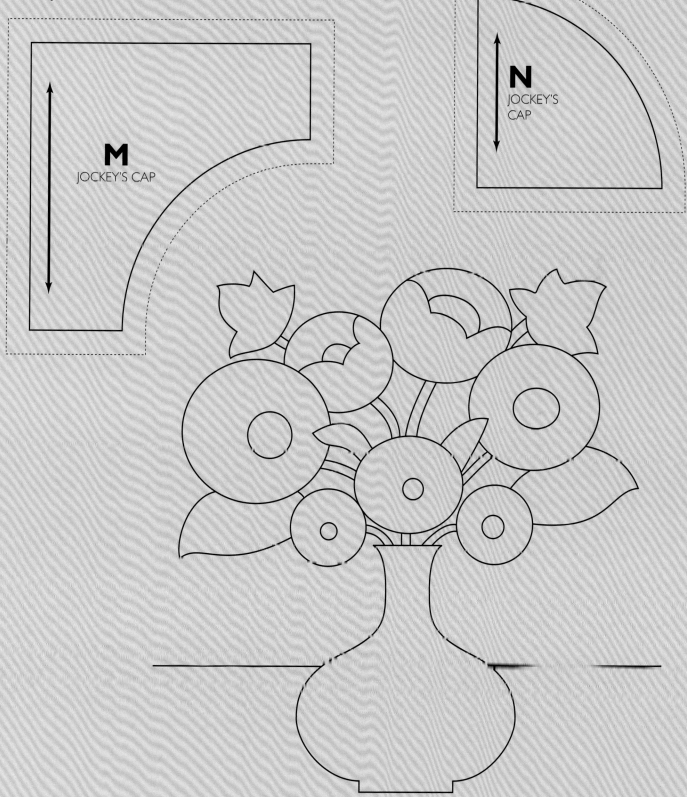

FOLK ART QUILT

The instructions for the *Folk Art Quilt* are on pages 105–107. The templates for the appliqué shapes are shown on this page and on pages 143–146 at 50 per cent of their actual size; enlarge 200 per cent for the correct size. Seam allowances are not needed on the appliqué because the raw edges are covered with stitching.

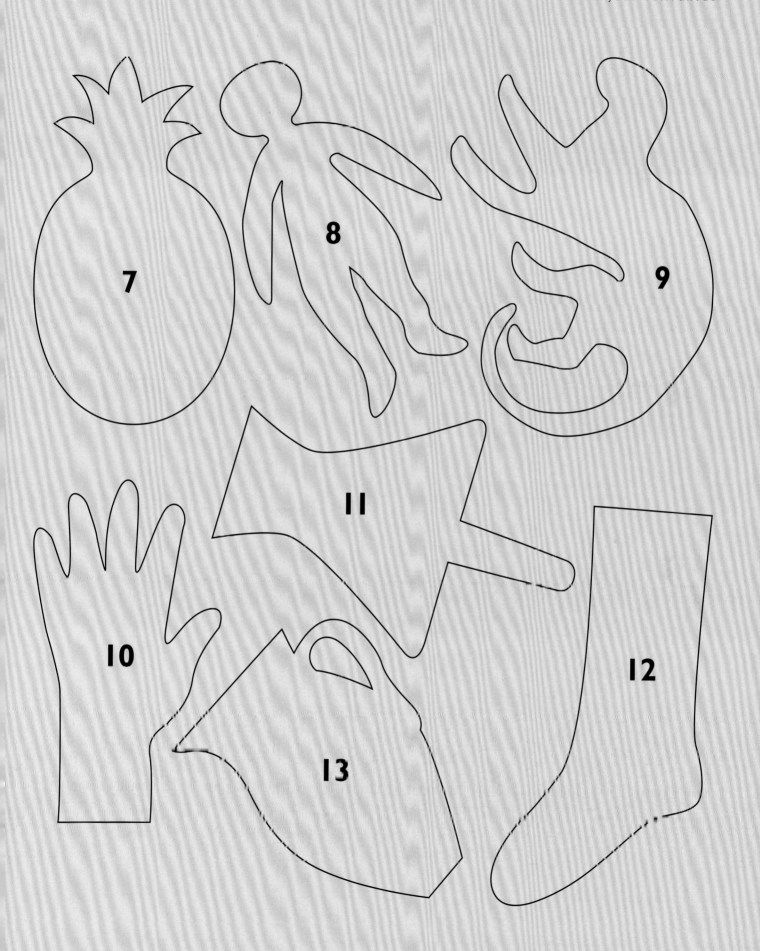

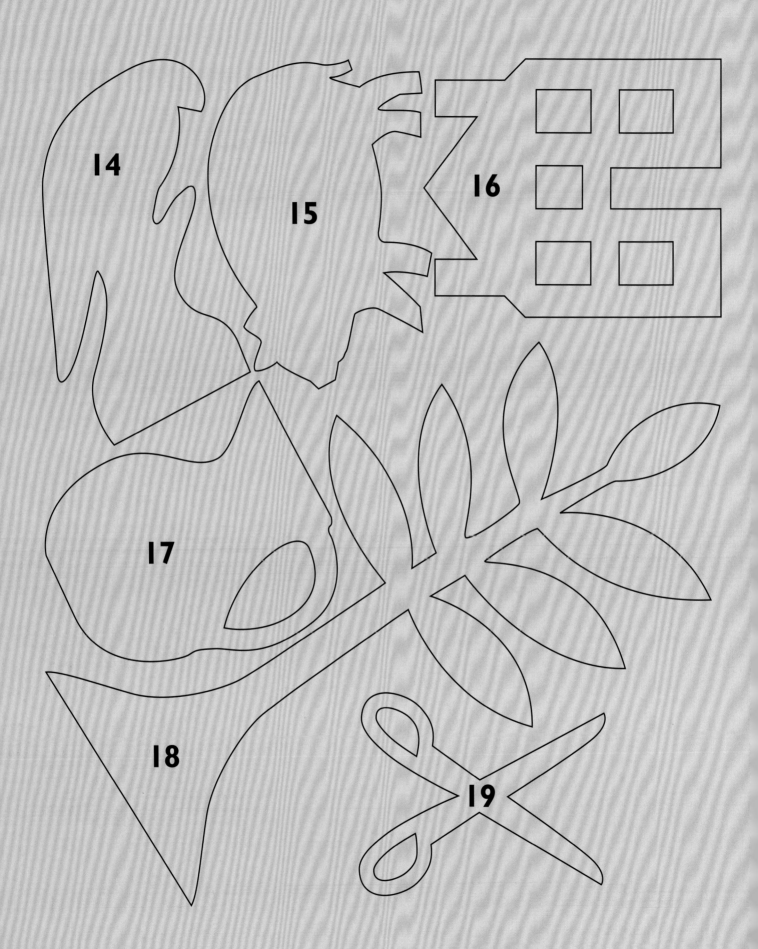

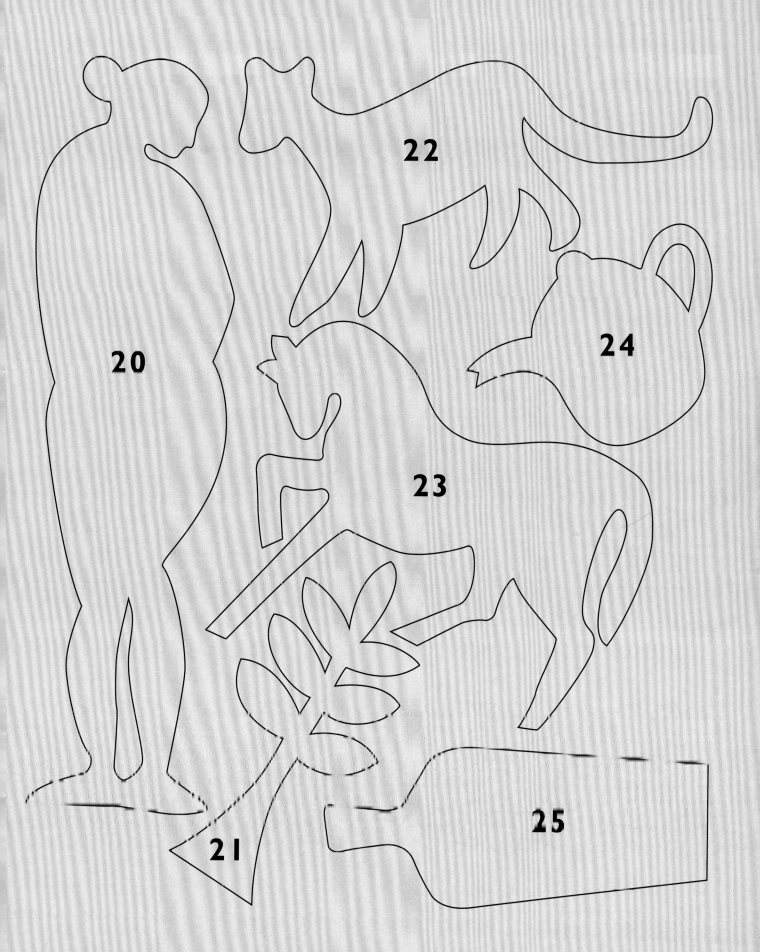

20

22

24

23

21

25

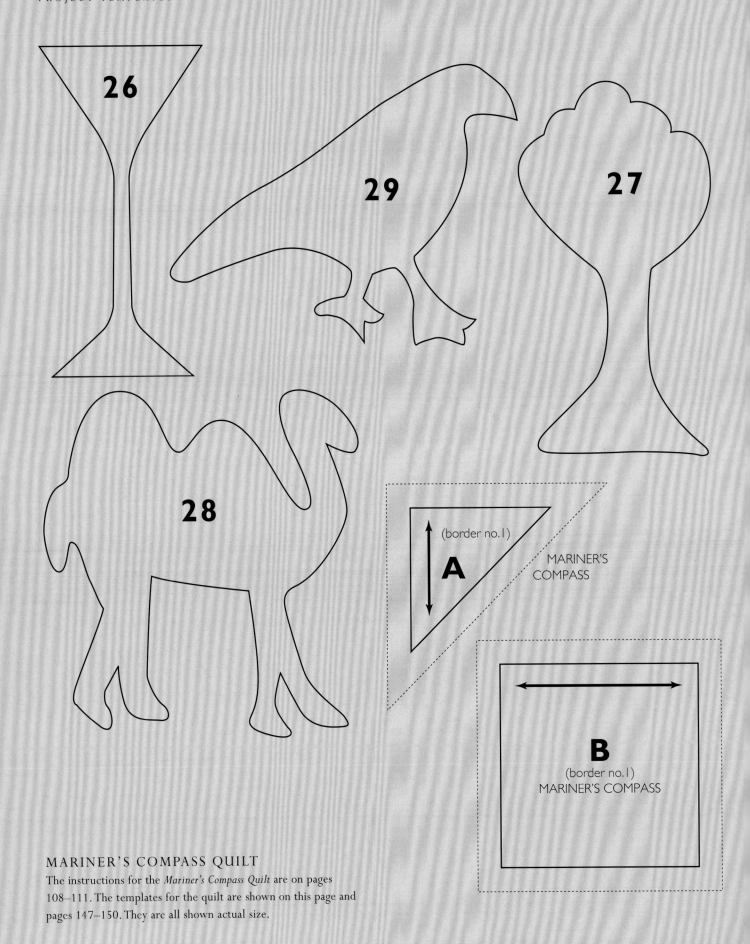

26

29

27

28

(border no.1)

A

MARINER'S
COMPASS

B
(border no.1)
MARINER'S COMPASS

MARINER'S COMPASS QUILT
The instructions for the *Mariner's Compass Quilt* are on pages
108–111. The templates for the quilt are shown on this page and
pages 147–150. They are all shown actual size.

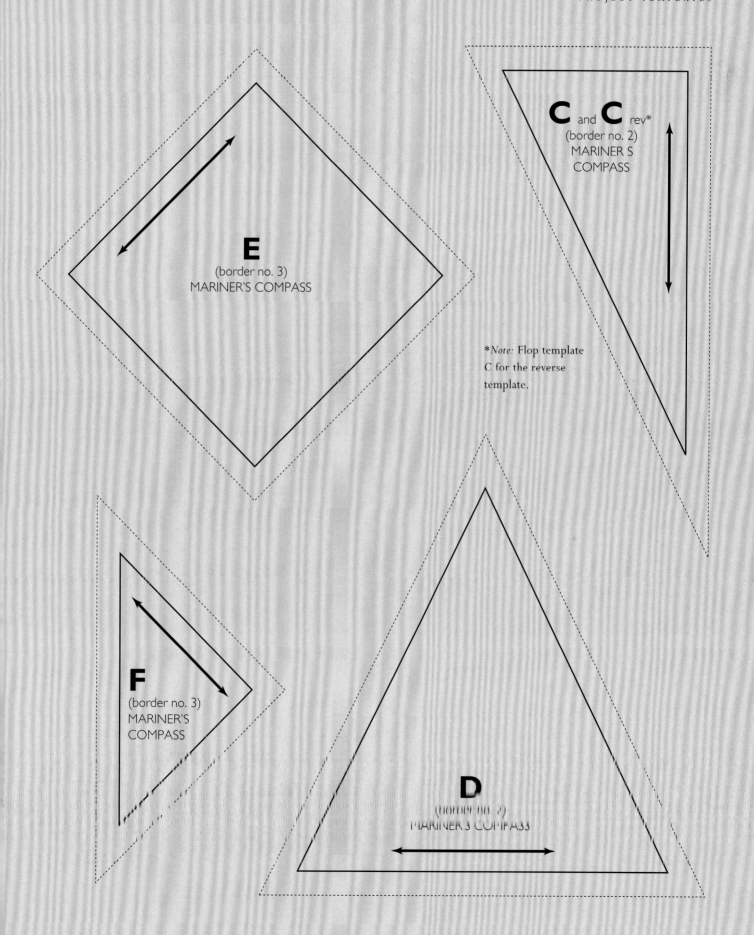

C and **C** rev*
(border no. 2)
MARINER S
COMPASS

E
(border no. 3)
MARINER'S COMPASS

Note: Flop template C for the reverse template.

F
(border no. 3)
MARINER'S
COMPASS

D
(border no. 2)
MARINER'S COMPASS

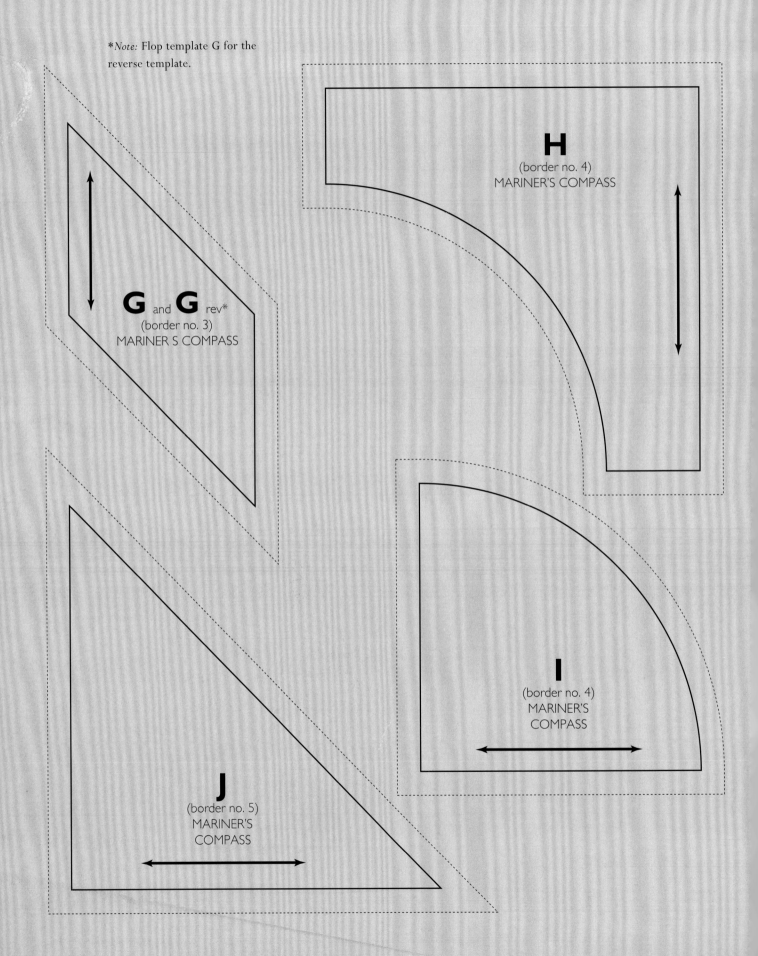

Note: Flop template G for the reverse template.

G and **G** rev*
(border no. 3)
MARINER S COMPASS

H
(border no. 4)
MARINER'S COMPASS

I
(border no. 4)
MARINER'S
COMPASS

J
(border no. 5)
MARINER'S
COMPASS

K
(border no. 6)
MARINER'S COMPASS

L and **L** rev*
(border no. 6)
MARINER S COMPASS

*Note: Flop template L for the reverse template.

MARINER'S COMPASS CENTRE

Use the template, on the left, for the paper foundation pieces that form the compass at the centre of the *Mariner's Compass Quilt*.

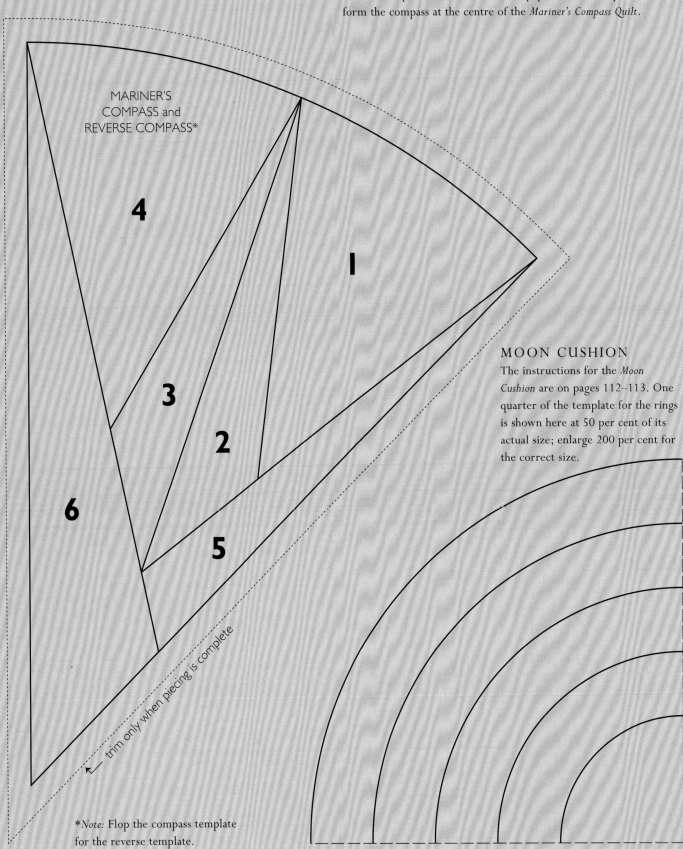

MARINER'S
COMPASS and
REVERSE COMPASS*

4

1

3

2

6

5

trim only when piecing is complete

MOON CUSHION

The instructions for the *Moon Cushion* are on pages 112–113. One quarter of the template for the rings is shown here at 50 per cent of its actual size; enlarge 200 per cent for the correct size.

Note: Flop the compass template for the reverse template.

SUN CUSHION

The instructions for the *Sun Cushion* are on pages 112–113. One quarter of the template for the paper foundation piece for the inner ring on the cushion is shown on the right; use this to make a full template for the inner ring. The template for the paper foundation piece for the outer ring is shown below; use this as instructed.

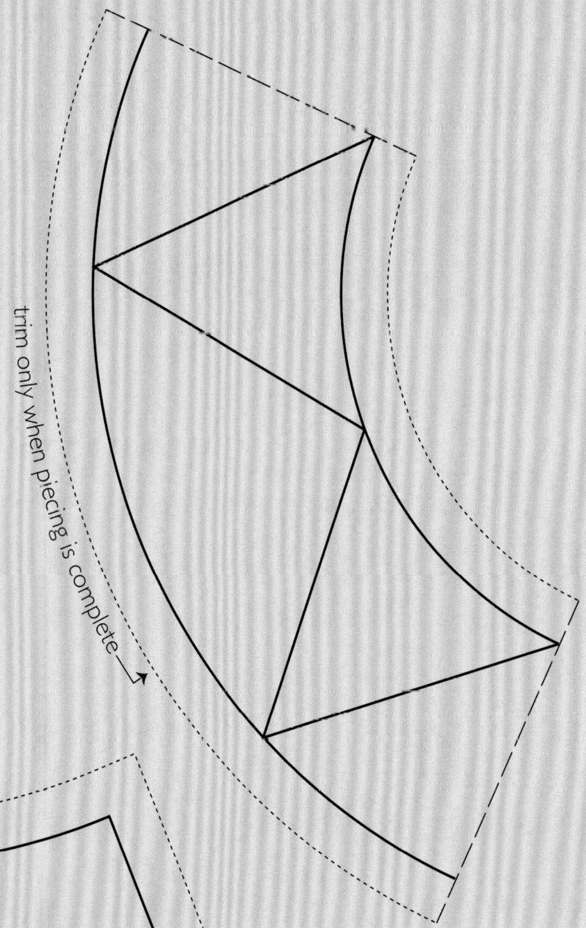

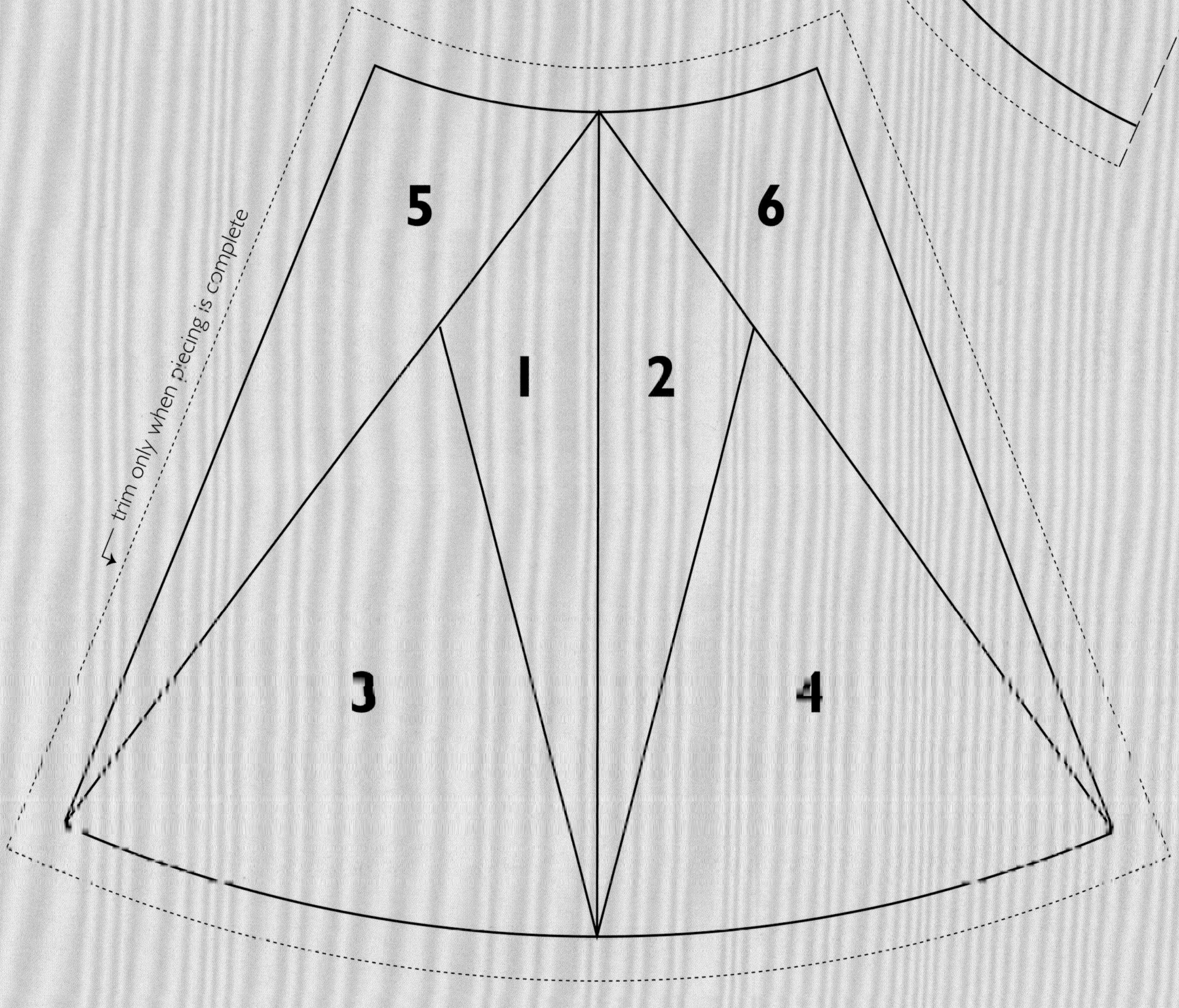

trim only when piecing is complete

trim only when piecing is complete

5

6

1

2

3

4

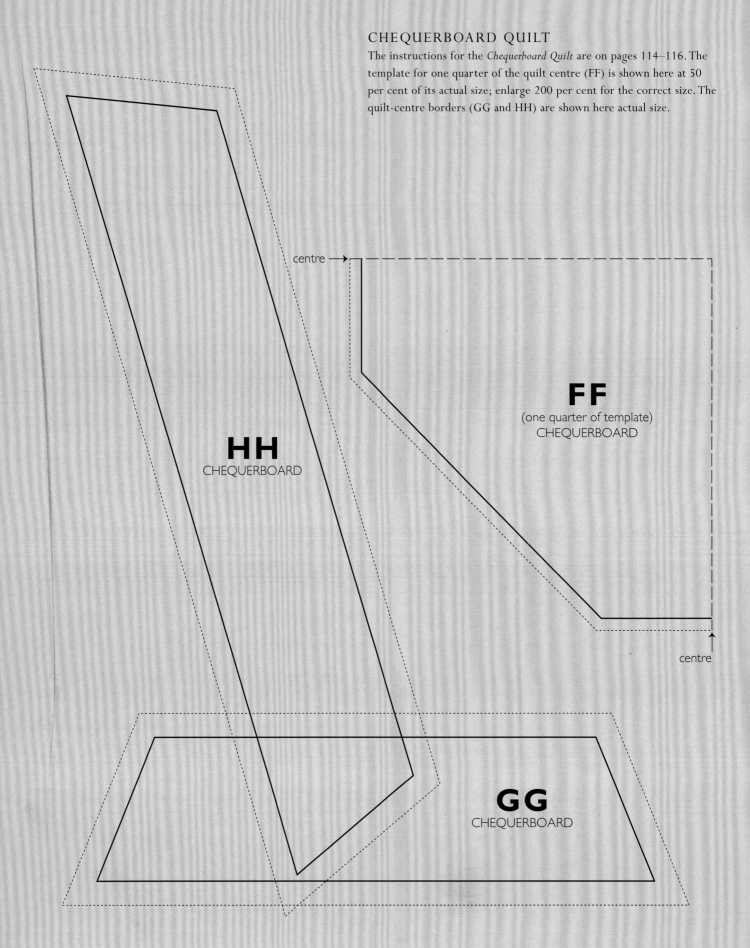

CHEQUERBOARD QUILT

The instructions for the *Chequerboard Quilt* are on pages 114–116. The template for one quarter of the quilt centre (FF) is shown here at 50 per cent of its actual size; enlarge 200 per cent for the correct size. The quilt-centre borders (GG and HH) are shown here actual size.

centre →

FF
(one quarter of template)
CHEQUERBOARD

centre

HH
CHEQUERBOARD

GG
CHEQUERBOARD

SAMPLER QUILT – BLOCKS 20, 38 AND 41

The instructions for the *Sampler Quilt* are on pages 117–121. The templates for blocks 20, 38 and 41 are shown here actual size. Only one quarter or one half of the template is shown, so you will need to flop the image, where necessary, to form the complete template. No seam allowances are given on these templates.

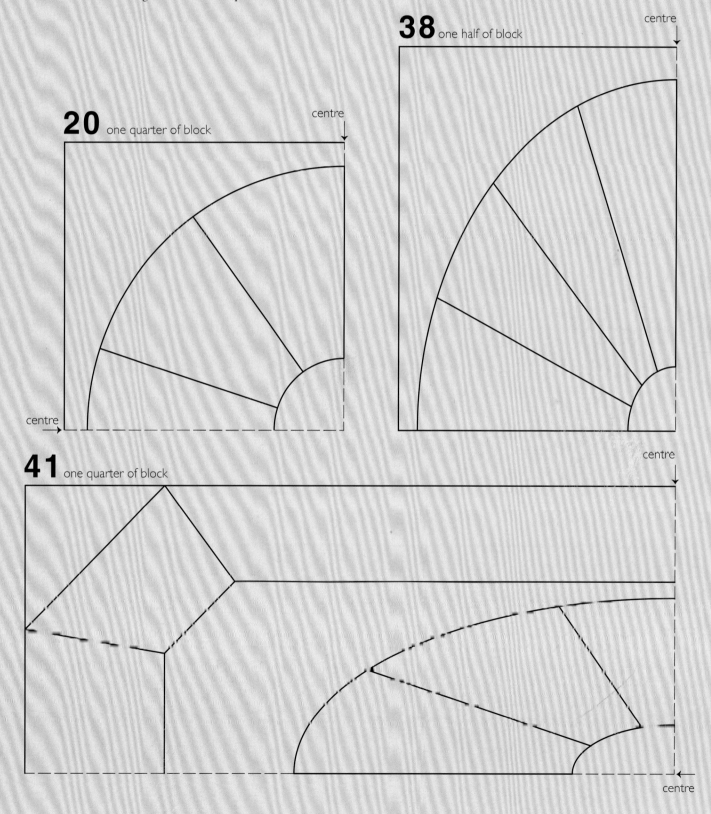

40 one half of block

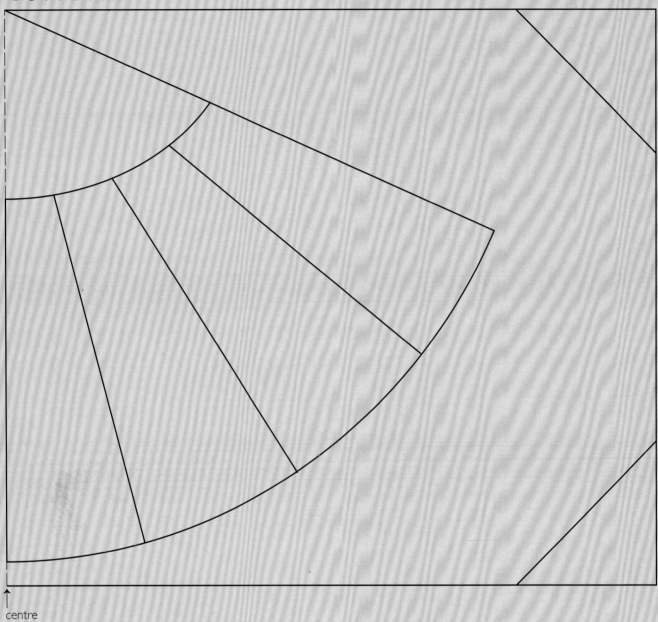

centre

SAMPLER QUILT – BLOCK 40

The template for block 40 of the *Sampler Quilt* is shown here actual size. Only one
half of the template is shown, so you will need to flop the image for the other half
to form the complete template. No seam allowances are given on this template. Cut
the background patch as a single piece. Use the fan shape with wedges as a paper
foundation piece and the centre circle shape as an appliqué template. Piece the
corner triangles onto the background.

42 one quarter of block (Dresden Flower)

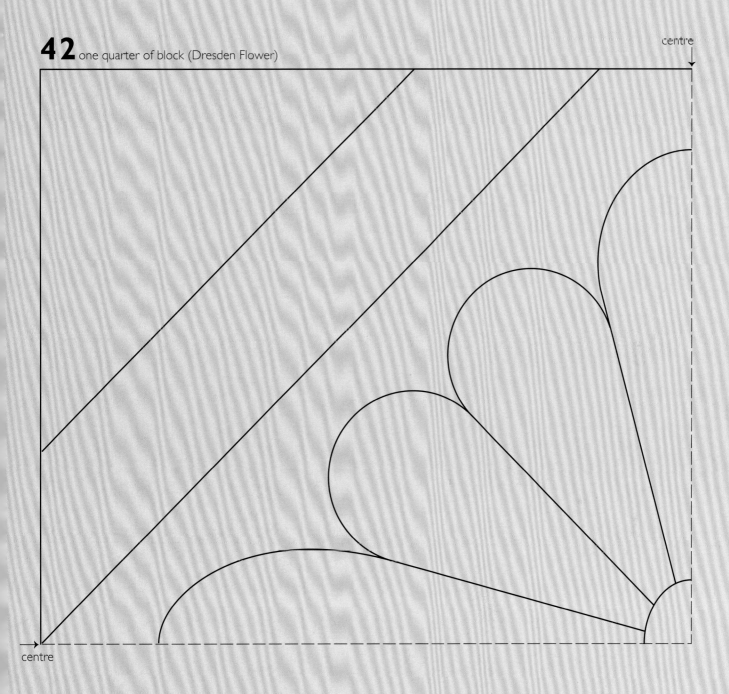

centre

centre

SAMPLER QUILT – BLOCK 42

The template for block 42 of the *Sampler Quilt* is shown here actual size.
Only one quarter of the template is shown, so you will need to flop the
image, where necessary, to form the complete template. No seam
allowances are given on this template. Use the petals and the centre circle
shape as appliqué templates. Piece the corner border strips and triangles
onto the large centre background patch.

43 one quarter of block (Dresden Plate)

centre

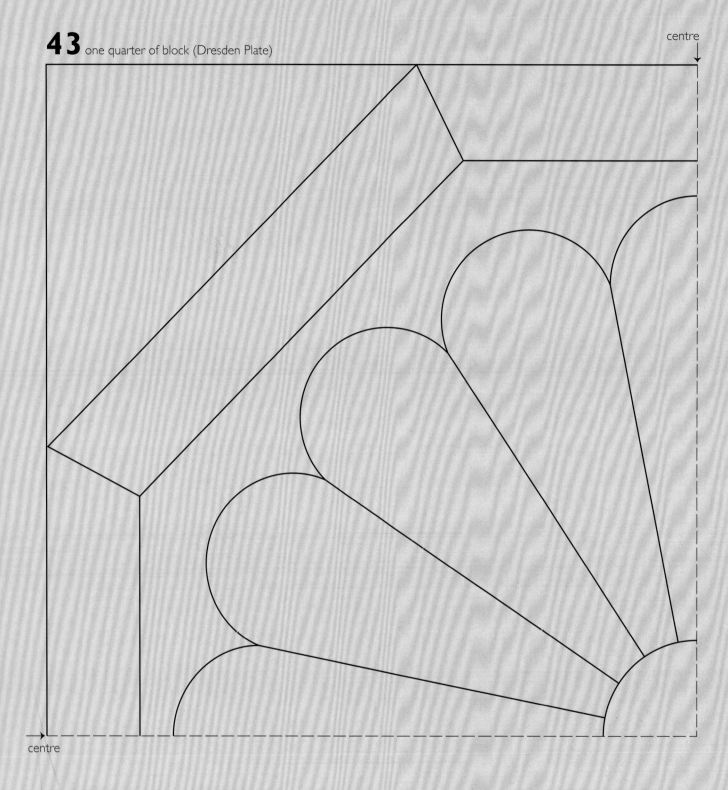

centre

SAMPLER QUILT – BLOCK 43

The template for block 43a of the *Sampler Quilt* is shown here actual size. Only one
quarter of the template is shown, so you will need to flop the image, where necessary,
to form the complete template. No seam allowances are given on this template. Use the
petal and the centre circle shape as appliqué templates. (The petal shapes are identical
so only one template is needed to trace the shape.) Use these appliqué shapes for blocks
½ 43 and 43b as well.

SAMPLER QUILT TEMPLATES

Most of the patch shapes for the *Sampler Quilt* are simple squares, rectangles and equilateral right-angled triangles, which can all be cut with simple cutting instructions (see Guide for Cutting Patches on page 118). A few patch shapes, however, need more complicated templates. Some of these templates can be taken from the partial blocks on pages 153–156, and the others are given on this page and the next. These templates are shown actual size, with the usual seam allowances.

Note: Flop templates HH and EE for the reverse templates.

HH and **HH** rev*
Block 18
SAMPLER
QUILT

AA
Block 5
SAMPLER QUILT

CC
Block 12
SAMPLER
QUILT

EE and
EE rev*
Block 16
SAMPLER
QUILT

BB
Block 6
SAMPLER QUILT

DD
Block 14
SAMPLER QUILT

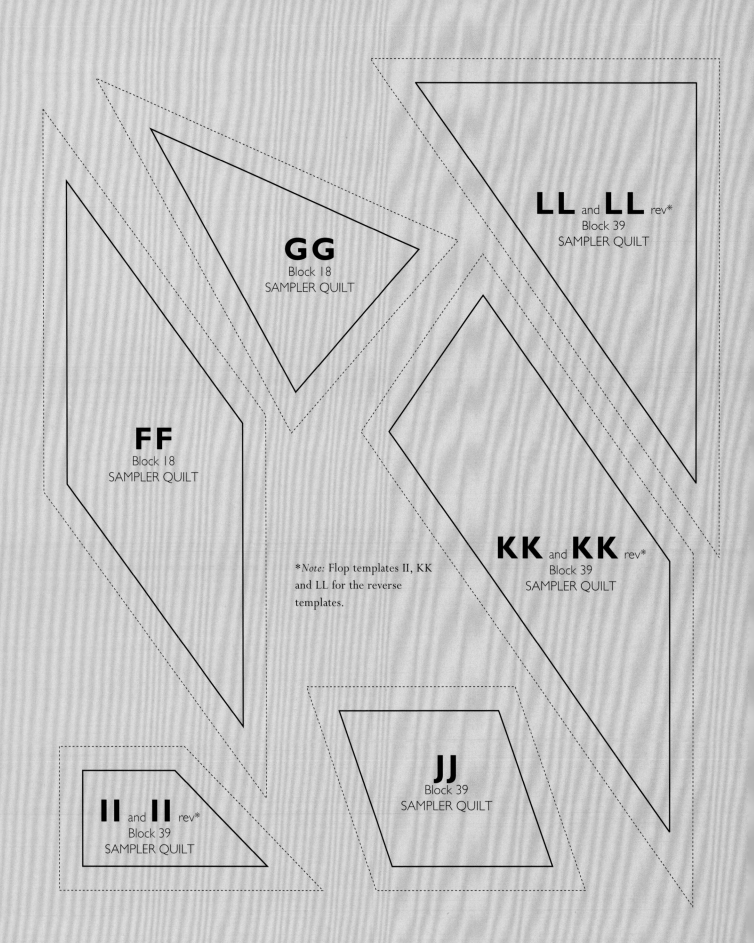

GG
Block 18
SAMPLER QUILT

LL and **LL** rev*
Block 39
SAMPLER QUILT

FF
Block 18
SAMPLER QUILT

KK and **KK** rev*
Block 39
SAMPLER QUILT

Note: Flop templates II, KK
and LL for the reverse
templates.

II and **II** rev*
Block 39
SAMPLER QUILT

JJ
Block 39
SAMPLER QUILT

AUTHORS' ACKNOWLEDGEMENTS

We are especially thankful to Judy Irish, whose beautiful quilting adds another dimension to all of our work.

Teaching quilt-making all over the world has had the added unexpected benefit of enabling us to make new friends with extraordinary quilters. We are grateful for the help they gave us in making these quilts. Thank you to Claudia Chaback for the *Lone Stars*. Thank you to Bekah Lynch for the *Winter Double Nine-Patch*. Thank you to Sandy MacKay, our expert compass maker. Thank you to Bobbi Penniman who helped with absolutely everything. And thanks to all of them for pitching in to help make the *Sampler Quilt*.

Thanks also to Sally Davis from the Quilt Connection in Berkeley Heights, New Jersey. This book began in the classroom of her store and with the able assistance of Alicia Bell, Kathy Bower, Alison Petersen and Patricia Smith. Thanks to Terry Clark for his wonderful quilting on the *Ode to Dale Evans* lone-star quilt. Nadine Shapiro's scissor work and Valerie Clarke's helpful hands with designing the *Folk Art Quilt* are appreciated.

A special thanks to Lil Nylen and her team at Husqvarna-Viking. The Designer I machine made sewing these quilts a real pleasure.

We are grateful to the folks at Electric Quilt for the wonderful software that made the pattern development a breeze.

We are grateful to Pauline Smith, Kathy Merrick and Andrea Graham, who helped us keep all the patchwork balls in the air.

At the V&A Museum, first, thanks to Linda Parry, whose book on patchwork started this off, and a special thanks to Susan North, who took time away from her textile department to show us the quilts – we think she was as tickled with the experience as we were. Thanks also to Mary Butler and the archive people who first showed us the V&A collection.

On the home front, writing, sewing, creating and travelling would not be possible without the help and encouragement of the entire Roos and Lucy families. Drew, Alex and Elizabeth Lucy live with more fabric and thread than a family ought. Their tolerance and love and computer skills have given us much appreciated support.

And next a big thank you to Debbie Patterson for our atmospheric room shots and Jon Stewart for flat shots, plus the V&A photo crew. Also to Sally Harding for the amazing job of editing this ever-changing gallery of quilts and to Chris Wood for her juicy design work and for making the book creation process so enjoyable.

Lastly, a great big thank you to Brandon Mably for co-ordinating this huge project from the nerve centre of our London Studio, and thanks to Kenneth and June Bridgewater and Joyce Robertson of Westminster Fibers and Stephen Sheard of Rowan for their belief and support.

PHOTO CREDITS

The publisher would like to thank the Victoria and Albert Museum, London, for the following photographs: page 2; pages 6–7; page 10; page 16, quilt T.124-1937; page 20, quilt T.417-1971; page 24, quilt T.117-1973; page 31, embroidery T.568-1996; page 32, bottom left, patchwork Circ. 273&A-1962; page 33; page 34, quilt T.76-1937; page 36, top, quilt T.99-1936; page 40, quilt T.154-1979; page 46, 242-1908; page 52, quilt T.19-1987; page 56, quilt T.428-1985; page 61, bottom, quilt T.86-1957; page 62, quilt T.154-1964; page 64, quilt T.9-1962; page 66, quilt T.17-1924; page 68, quilt T.102-1938.

SUPPLIERS OF KAFFE FASSETT FABRICS

To find out where to buy Kaffe Fassett patchwork fabrics near you, contact one of the following addresses.

UK AND WORLDWIDE
Rowan Yarns
Green Lane Mill
Holmfirth
West Yorkshire
HD9 7DX
England
Tel: +44 (0) 1484 681881
Fax: +44 (0) 1484 687920
E-mail: mail@knitrowan.com

USA AND CANADA
Westminster Fibers, Inc
18 Celina Avenue, Unit 17
Nashua, NH 03063
USA
Tel: 1-800-445-9276 or
603-459-2441 x 203
Fax: 603-459-2444
E-mail: fabrics@westminsterfibers.com

INDEX